BACK ON THE COURT

A Young Woman's Triumphant Return
to
Life, Love and Basketball

by
Sonya G. Elliott

A Tigress Publishing Book

ISBN: 978-1-59404-045-0
Library of Congress Control Number: 2011934567
Printed in the United States of America

Book Design: Steve Montiglio
Editor: Peter Atkins
Cover Photo: Rudy Loupias

10 9 8 7 6 5 4 3 2 1

For
Jason, Charli and Cass

In memory of
Mark Alan Overholt

PROLOGUE

"I can't wait to be Mrs. Overholt," I say, squeezing Mark's hand tight in mine as we step off the basketball court. "Just a few more days and we'll be man and wife."

A dimple accompanies Mark's smile as he releases my hand and gives me a playful pat on the butt before we sit down to change out of our high-tops. I know I've made the right decision to marry Mark. He's everything I want in a man, in a lover, in a husband. For the rest of my life.

"Let's get out of here," Mark says, popping to his feet. Offering me his outstretched hand, he lures me with his sparkling green eyes and the turned-up corners of his lips as he draws me to him for a kiss. We gather our things and stroll out of the gym hand-in-hand. I am in heaven.

It's dusk as we make our way to the far side of the parking lot. When I walk around Mark's black Prelude to the passenger door the darkening night moves up behind Mark like a thick fog. I can barely see him across the roof of the car as he searches his duffle for keys. The darkness creeps closer to him, swallowing everything in its path. As Mark leans down, I lose sight of him and my throat tightens. A cool dampness fills the air. I move around the car but by the time I reach the driver's side, he has disappeared.

"Mark?" I say. The darkness surrounds my body and I run my hand along the car to find the door, to find Mark. He is not there. The hair on the back of my neck electrifies. I reach out my hands, searching for him. I call through the darkness, "Mark! Mark!" The darkness grows thicker, holding me back until it swallows me. "MARK! Where are you, Mark! Mark!" I am wrapped in total darkness and, except for my pounding heart, there is silence. In the distance, I hear a faint beep and a tiny light flickers for a split-second before darkness returns.

The beeping continues, getting louder and more intense. There's another flash of light. Mark, where are you? My chest sinks under a heavy weight. Pain radiates from my heart to every part of my body. Every organ, every limb, every bone reverberates with pain that builds like a wave, growing stronger and stronger. Mark I need you; where are you? Pain overwhelms my whole being. With the beep I hear a voice. The voice pierces the distance. My name, someone is calling my name. Mark is that you? I try desperately to listen.

"Sonya?"

Mark? I want to ask but find that I cannot speak.

"Sonya, can you hear me?" The muffled words reach me.

My eyelids lift with tremendous effort but then drop like heavy weights. The flash of light fades. I must open my eyes. My eyelids lift again. The light burns. I let my eyes close.

"Sonya, we're right here," says another voice, this one lower.

Mark, is that you? Oh please, I need you. My eyelids lift once more and this time stay open long enough to make out the faces of those talking to me. Mom? Dad? My eyes close again. Where is Mark?

I open my eyes and focus as best as I can against the awful brightness and the pain. There's more beeping. It's close by.

2

I hear another sound, as though someone is sucking air in through their teeth and back out again. It's louder with every breath and I want it to stop. My head is pounding. I open my eyes once more and though my sight is blurry, I am stricken by what I see. My parents are looking down at me.

"Sonya, we're right here."

Their faces seem tense. My eyes close again. Mom touches my hand.

"We love you," she says. I feel a gentle squeeze.

I open my eyes and then gasp from the pain. "Where's Mark?" I shut my eyes. I can hardly breathe. As I open my eyes one more time, I force the words across my lips. "Tell me please, is Mark okay?"

"You're going to be okay," my mom answers.

I close my eyes. The pain overwhelms me.

"Where...is...Mark?" I gasp.

"It's going to be okay, you're going to be okay." A second hand, my father's, touches my arm.

"Where is Mark?" I try again, panic filling my body and mind.

Beeping sounds echo throughout the room. The whooshing fills my ears and the pain fills my entire being.

"I'm so sorry." My mom leans closer, her grip on my hand tightening. Her voice contracts and her tears spill on my arm. "You've been in an accident," she whispers, the words barely able to leave her mouth, "You've been badly hurt."

"What about Mark?" I cry.

My whole body begins to shake uncontrollably and I think the pain will shatter me forever. I try to open my eyes, but the light is too bright, too blinding, too terrible.

PART I
February 1991 — Seattle, Washington

FOR THE LOVE OF THE GAME

Shielding my eyes from the bright overhead lights, I lie with my back against the hardwood floor and place my hand on the soft leather ball that rests by my side. I breathe in and fill my lungs completely with air, then pick up the ball and run my hand over the narrow rubber ridges that divide the ball into eight equal parts. I exhale and, by instinct, my fingertips search for the ridge that will lead to a perfect backspin. I open my eyes, push myself off the floor, and slide the basketball under my arm.

Waiting on the sideline with the ball held lightly against my hip, I feel tall. And when I step onto the court and guide the ball gently from my hip to the floor for the next game, my game, I am ready for competition. I'm playing pickup ball with the guys at Shoreline Gym. I have played basketball in many gyms: Notre Dame, where I played in the national AAU tournament; Adams Field House, where my college team beat the Lady Griz to advance to the NCAA playoffs; and Eastern Washington University's Reese Court, where I spent four years of my life pounding the hardwoods. All gyms, even the small ones where I now coach and play pickup ball, have the same black lines and two ten-foot orange hoops, but each has a character and memory all its own.

Shoreline is one of many open gyms I have discovered since graduating from college and moving to Seattle three years ago. Monday-night games here happen to be my favorite. On Wednesdays I like to play at Ravenna-Eckstein Community Center. Tuesdays and Thursdays I go to Green Lake, and when I'm in need of another game, I go to the University of Washington's IMA as a last resort (because there's often more arguing than basketball). Counting my league games, I play at least five days a week, and if it's a good week, I play more.

As a woman, getting on a court is generally a bigger challenge than the competition itself, and today is no different. I need to get on the court quickly because I have a league game across town in Queen Anne that starts in two hours. Why drive 20 minutes north to play basketball for an hour and then drive south another 20 minutes to play again? I simply love to play basketball; it's my passion.

When I was almost one, my parents watched as I sat barefoot in the grass and all alone pushed myself to standing and walked for the very first time. Not long after, my preparations as a ballplayer began as I spent my days trying to keep up with my brother Putz who was three years older and six years bigger. We were an active family, but when it came to playing basketball I started with a blank slate. My dad is Austrian. He played fussball (the soccer kind); basketball isn't in his repertoire. My mom, who grew up in Montana, was trained to sing opera. She would feel right at home singing the national anthem, but would have no idea what to do on the court. Still, my family made its way through cold Montana winters to watch a lot of Grizzly basketball at the University of Montana, and for that I am thankful.

One night in particular, I remember plunking myself on the hard bleachers between my mom and Putz. I tucked my hands, palms down, under my thighs, leaned forward, and stared intently at the game. As I watched the players make their way up and down the court with the ball, my heart began to pound. I knew – for certain – I was looking at my future. When the whistle blew, I poked my mom's arm with my tiny finger.

"Mom, I want to play basketball."

Mom turned, peered at me through the bottom of her large round-framed glasses, and said, "They don't have basketball for girls your age, Sonya."

"Oh," I said, my eyes narrowing as I looked back to the court with a heavy heart, then added under my breath, "That's not fair."

Resting a hand on my shoulder, my mom hesitated then replied, "That doesn't mean you can't play."

Not long after, Dad hoisted an old railroad tie vertically, cemented it in to the ground, and attached a backboard and hoop so Putz and I could toss a basketball around with the kids in the neighborhood. And tossing, not shooting, was what we did with no one to coach us. That was the beginning of my love affair with the game.

I was busy during high school; I excelled in athletics but also spent the years hoping a boy might notice me, might see beyond my buckteeth, knock knees and sandy blonde hair that wouldn't feather just right. Later, at Eastern Washington University, when boys did begin to notice me, I learned to appreciate but ignore their admiring glances and retreat into my world of basketball and school. I carried eighteen to twenty credits a quarter and traveled with the basketball team. And then, after interviewing a modeling agency for a class project my junior year, I threw modeling into the mix. Four years passed quickly and after graduating with honors I packed my Volkswagen Rabbit and moved to Seattle to model. My parents thought I should put my Communication degree to better use, but I figured modeling would be a good way to make money and travel. I started modeling right away, and though I had to supplement my income by waiting tables, I was happy.

Glancing across to the far court this evening, a new player catches my eye. With a hesitation dribble he moves swiftly around his defender, and takes the ball to the hoop. He gently lays the ball against the backboard, and as it drops through the net, he makes a quick pivot and sprints down on defense. A smile flickers on his lips and his eyes narrow as his opponent dribbles the ball back up the court. I stop dribbling, and for the first time in a long while, my mind isn't on basketball.

I haven't really noticed a man since my college boyfriend and I split up. But this man, with his strong build, thick dark hair, and smiling emerald eyes has an unguarded confidence that demands my full attention. As he glides effortlessly up and down the court, he hypnotizes me with his command of the game. When the game on the court in front of me ends, my heart sinks, realizing I won't get the chance to play against him.

I step onto the hardwoods to play. I'm matched with a tall guard who likes to drive to the hoop, so I work hard to take away his drive and block him off the boards. Occasionally, I glance to the far court where the young man is playing, but as I fall into the comfort of my game, I play and enjoy what I have come for: the workout, the competition, and the energy that comes from being where I'm not expected to be. I get a charge from being a woman who looks, to most people, not at all like a basketball player, though I have Division 1 college basketball experience and can mix it up with anyone on the court. Today I hope this "toughness," as well as my long blonde hair and slender build, might catch the attention of the young man who has caught mine.

When my game ends, I hurry to the sideline and gather my gear. Not once have I made eye contact with the handsome man, but as I turn to take one last look, there he is, right smack in front of me, his hand reaching out to mine.

"Hi! I'm Mark," he says in a strong clear voice.

"I'm Sonya," I answer, noticing his firm hand shake.

"You're a great player."

"Thanks," I say, my cheeks hot and my heart racing.

"You play here much?"

"Most Mondays," I answer, glancing at the clock, "I hate to be rude, but I've got to hurry to get to my game."

I sit down to take off my high tops.

"What?" Mark looks at me as I stuff my high tops into my duffle bag. "You have a game now?"

"Yeah, I play in a women's league Monday nights," I say, standing up and throwing my bag over my shoulder, "and I'm late."

Mark follows as I jog to the door. I hesitate in the doorway, turning to admire his questioning eyes one last time before I leave.

"Good luck!" he says.

"Thanks," I smile, then turn and run to my car.

A week later I can see Mark's smiling eyes in my mind while I drive to Shoreline's gym on Monday night. It's been a long week wondering if I will see him again, and I decide that, if I do, I will ask him out for a quick beer before my league game. When I arrive at the gym he is nowhere in sight. I sit down and slowly tie each shoe, periodically glancing to the door. Over the last week I have imagined what it would be like to be with Mark, to have his strong arms pull me tight against his broad chest, to have his lips pressed against mine, but now I might never see him again. The fact that I care kind of bothers me. Damn it, I don't want to see Mark. I tuck my street shoes into my bag. I like my freedom. I pick up my ball and look for a team that doesn't have five players. The teams are full so I ask around, gathering a new team of five.

"Hey Sonya, you wanna take my spot?" Allan, a friend and fellow gym rat, calls across the court. "I've gotta get going."

"Sure." I put my ball next to my duffle bag and run onto the court to meet my team.

"Hi, I'm Sonya." I reach my hand out to a couple of guys I don't know, before I move to the wing position.

Everyone on the court matches up to guard a player from the opposing team, and because we are the winning team, our team starts with the ball. One guy, whose shirt is tattered from undoubtedly too many long nights of partying, stands at the point, but his defender won't give up the ball to start the game. Instead he turns to me and says, "How about you guys go skins." Everybody laughs. I consider taking off my top for shock value. After all, I am wearing a sports bra under my shirt. But instead I simply smile as the opposing players take off their shirts and toss them to the sidelines.

"If I had a dime for every time I've heard that," I say as I jog down to stack with the low post.

The game begins and I cut around the post for the ball. I pass it back to the point, set a pick down low then cross to the opposite block, taking hard hits as defenders fight through the screens. I pop out to the opposite wing and get the pass on the reversal, just in time to put in a quick jumper. Wanting to smile at the man who made the "skins" comment, I smile to myself instead, and back-pedal down the court on defense. I revel in my ability to play tough defense and crash the boards, and as a rule, I usually wait to shoot the ball, but after his comment, I couldn't help myself.

Calling for the outlet, I push the ball up the court and hit a man on the breakaway for a lay-in, then sprint down the court again on defense. Working to hold my man to low numbers, I play with an intensity that is heightened by the possibility of seeing Mark again. As the ball moves up and down the court, my eyes occasionally wander toward the gym door and I have nearly given up hope when Mark strolls in. My chest tightens when I remember my decision to ask him out for beers and I try to calm myself by bringing my mind back to the game.

I look over and smile at Mark as I run up the court. He leans against the wall, crosses his arms, and watches. Knowing he's looking, I amp up my game. Finally the game ends and the next team of five steps onto the court. Mark is one of them. He takes off his sweats. Under his sweatshirt he has on a white cotton t-shirt with a blue Nike across the chest. On his face he is wearing a broad smile.

"I've got her," he says, bringing his lips together while looking me in the eye.

"Grrreat," I reply, returning his smile.

Playing basketball against a man tells me more about him than any date. I get to know the real Mark. He doesn't give me a break. He takes me to the hoop, crashes the boards, and even steals one of my passes. He uses his body to move me out of the way and get a loose ball, and then flashes a smile in my direction. Mark captures my heart with his intensity and teamwork each time down the court and my admiration is deepened by the chance to be near him. His unmistakable masculine scent is enhanced by the warmth of his body and becomes permanently ingrained in my mind as we move on the court together. I crave it like chocolate. I wish the game would never end.

When it does, Mark stops to talk with a teammate on his way up the sidelines. I leave the court and sit down to change my shoes. While he talks, I study his muscular legs, the curve that brings his hamstring to meet the back of his knee, the definition in his thick calves. As he shifts his weight the muscles flicker and flex. I remember my decision to ask him for a beer.

I don't have much time before my league game, I better just get going. I finish tying my shoes, then gathering my things; I walk slowly to the door.

"Would you like to go to a Sonics game on Wednesday?" says a voice over my shoulder.

I turn and once again find myself face to face with Mark.

"I'd love to," I say.

"Great! What's your phone number?"

"Here," I answer, searching for a pen and piece of paper in my bag. "I'm headed to play a game right now, but you can call me later tonight or anytime tomorrow."

I hand him a crumpled receipt with my name and number written on it.

"I'll call tonight," he says.

Looking out my apartment window Wednesday evening I watch each car pass. It's been a long time since I've been on a date. My last boyfriend and I had been together for seven years. I am used to hanging out with guys, but going on a date is a different story. A dark Honda Prelude pulls into a parking space in front of my apartment, and out jumps Mark with an energy that I will soon learn is an integral part of his being.

We start the evening with dinner at Dukes on Lake Union, where he opens the door and leads me into a room with blue and white checkered tablecloths and TV screens everywhere, perfect for a casual night of basketball. The conversation is aimed in my direction when Mark asks about my family. I tell him about my mom and dad and how they own a German delicatessen in Spokane. I tell him about my grandma and grandpa, whom I call Honey and Bampa and about my big brother Putz, whom I jokingly call my little brother. He is 6' 3" and looks like Arnold Schwarzenegger.

I tell Mark about my best friends, Leslie and Kirsten –

how we met in junior high and remain friends, though we live far apart. I don't tell him that Leslie and Kirsten were band geeks and loved the bookmobile. I also don't mention that we were honor students, didn't drink alcohol in high school, and, according to our classmates, were total nerds.

Mark's eyes dance as he tells me about his family. He has three younger sisters. The youngest, Debbie, will turn twenty-one soon. Mark has been saving dimes in a big glass jar to pay for a limo to take her out on the town for her birthday, like he's done for his other two sisters, Wendy and Vikki. I'm impressed. I can't imagine anyone investing in a 21st birthday limo for one sister, let alone three. As Mark shares more stories, I can tell how important family is to him. How all of them are a huge part of his life. I like what I hear.

"Gramma and Grandpa are the best, they still come to most of my rec-league baseball games," he proudly admits.

"That's awesome."

"Yeah, I'm pretty lucky."

"I'd love to meet them," I say, dabbing a thick fry into the ketchup.

"They live on Vashon, but I think they're coming to my parents' house this weekend," he says, never letting his gaze leave mine. "Maybe you could come to my parents for dinner on Saturday? My sisters might be there too."

"It sounds like fun," I answer with a calm that masks my hesitation at meeting the entire family at once.

Mark continues, "You could come to my apartment and we could drive to my parents in Everett together."

"That would be great, but I need to check what shifts I'm working this weekend," I say before taking another bite.

By the time we finish mud pie, I know that Mark is twenty-four years old, has a new job as an insurance adjuster, has a new apartment near Northgate, graduated from the University of

Puget Sound (where he played baseball), and that he loves to play basketball. I also know I will find someone to cover my shift Saturday night.

Not wanting to miss tip-off, Mark pays the bill and we run hand-in-hand to the car. After struggling to find a parking spot we pull against the curb on a street far from the stadium and start walking. Should I ask Mark if he remembered the tickets? I'm afraid to ask, afraid of seeming like a nag, but as we enter the crosswalk, I can't help myself.

"Have you got the tickets?" I say, and give a sheepish grin.

Mark looks at me, cocks his head to the side, checks both pockets, and runs back to the car. Returning, he grabs my hand and we hurry to tip-off. I spent seven years of my life pretending to be someone other than myself in my last relationship. With Mark, something tells me I can be myself, nerd and all.

After cheering the Sonics to a win, Mark and I continue celebrating into the night. When we return to my apartment in the heart of the University District the streets are dark and still. My fingers are held snug in Mark's hand as he walks me to the door. When we reach the door and he turns to face me, to look into my eyes, I know he will kiss me. My heart is pounding. He lets go of my hand and gently caresses my cheek. We draw closer and as our lips touch we wrap our arms around one another, holding each other tight. Short of breath, I ask Mark if he would like to come in.

We see one another every day after our first date. Every day becomes every night. I alter my shifts waiting tables to be with him and after one sleep-deprived month together, I feel a comfort and security I've never known.

James Taylor plays softly in the background while I stretch. I sit on the floor after my run, body bent over extended leg, and stare at the sunlight that spreads across the speckled

Berber carpet of my new rooftop apartment – an apartment I moved into last week to have a place of my own. I imagine Mark's hand gently pushing my hair behind my ear before he touches his lips to my cheek, my ear, my neck. He whispers, "Sonya, I love you. I want to spend the rest of my life with you." There is an ache in the pit of my stomach. I have fallen for him. I can imagine marrying him. In fact we spoke of marriage last week, after being together one month and now I'm scared. Marriage? I just got out of a long and serious relationship. Brianna, my cat, steps across my leg and runs her nose against my hand. I run my fingers along her soft fur before I sink lower onto my leg. I think about getting married, about a wedding. Even while stretching, tension spreads through my body. I switch legs. I need to think about what is right for me. I love Mark, but I'm afraid of loving him so much, too soon. I need to slow things down.

My thoughts are interrupted by footsteps ascending the scaffolding-like stairwell that attaches to the outside of the three-story 1920's house, the top floor of which is my small studio apartment. The footsteps stop just as a quick rap comes at the door.

Before I move, the door swings open and Mark steps in holding a bouquet of red roses tight in his hand.

"Wow!" I say, standing up slowly.

He has already given me an expensive Elton John boxed set for no special reason and now this.

Reaching for the roses, I lean to give him a quick kiss then turn to look for a vase.

"What's up?" Mark asks, questioning the ever-so-brief kiss.

"Nothing," I answer adjusting the stems in an oversized Mason jar.

Mark walks behind me, and encompasses my body with his arms.

"What's wrong?" he tries again, giving me a gentle squeeze.

I can't speak and stand for a long time, quiet in his arms. He can't see my tears, but I taste them as they drip into my mouth just before I say the unthinkable.

"Mark," I begin, then turn in his arms to face him, "maybe we're taking this too fast."

"What?" he says, his eyes narrowing. "Do you want to break up?"

"I don't know," I answer looking down. "I mean, we've talked about marriage, and I just don't know if I'm ready for that."

"Well, you love me, don't you?" he asks, picking up my chin to look me in the eye.

"Yes," I answer, eyebrows lifted.

He smiles, bringing my face to his chest before he wraps me with his arms. We stay this way for a long time, the heat of our bodies making my mind whirl.

Finally Mark steps back and reaches into his coat pocket, pulls out a white envelope and places it gently in my hand. I open the envelope and read Mark's poem.

How Is Her Touch So Different?

I ask,
How can this be so different?
The touch of her hand,
A kiss on my neck.

Now I see,
There are two sides to this coin.
The sensation of touch,
But with a feeling of love.

Love Mark

Cheeks still wet with tears, I laugh as he kisses me on the

forehead.

"Well then," he says, grabbing both my arms and holding me away from his body as he looks me in the eye, "don't let a good thing go."

I can't help but smile too, and as I wrap my arms around Mark and sink my face into his chest once more, I understand that it is okay to be scared. I thought I couldn't want anything more than the life I was already living, my life of basketball and freedom. But I was wrong. Mark and I have a great thing going, and I see now that I will never let him go.

A DOZEN REASONS

As the days pass Mark and I talk about spending the rest of our lives together. We talk about our family, our Mark and Sonya Overholt family. Mark wants to have enough kids for a basketball team; I argue for a healthy pair, any shape or size. We toss around the idea of saving for a house by moving in together and managing an apartment complex. We talk more about getting married.

Our wedding, according to Mark, will be a big Catholic affair. I'm not Catholic, but as long as I don't have to convert and we will spend our lives together as man and wife, it sounds good to me. I want a simple wedding with no hints of the color pink, ruffles or other "kitschig" (my family's German term for tacky) decorations. There will be plenty of food and wine, and of course music, music to keep even our grandparents swinging and swaying through the night.

The only thing we don't talk about is when we will actually do this, get married. When we will get engaged for that matter? It is understood, of course, but now I want Mark to ask me, for us to set a date. We have a weekend visit with Mark's grandparents planned on Vashon Island. I've spent a lot of time with them, cheering for Mark during his fast-pitch softball tournaments, and I look forward to spending time with them at their home. But more importantly, Vashon is special to Mark and I hope that it might become special to me as well, that he might ask me to marry him there.

When Mark comes to pick me up in a sparkling clean car and his smile is a bit brighter than usual, I suspect I might be right. Mark meets me half way up the bony wooden staircase that leads to my apartment, gives me a kiss then grabs my bag and hustles back down to place it in the back of his Honda. As he opens my door, I steal a kiss and scoot into my seat. In moments we're driving south on Highway 99, humming along with Smokey Robinson as the Space Needle towers over us in the cloudless sky on our way to the Vashon ferry. Traffic slows to a stop near the north end of Lincoln Park, and as we pull onto the loading dock to wait in line neither of us speaks. We simply listen to Smokey's smooth voice inviting us to see the future in each other's eyes.

I search Mark's eyes, and then give him a long kiss before leaning back and sinking into the bucket seat. As I absorb the sunlight, I'm entranced by the shimmering rays as they touch the crest of each and every ripple of water. Mark, now deep in thought, holds a steady gaze out the window as well. He aimlessly moves something from hand to hand and as he slips his hand into his jacket, a shimmer like that on the waves flashes from between his fingers. My chest tightens and as I turn my face to his, he gives me a soft smile and pulls his hand from inside his jacket.

"This is going to be an awesome weekend," he says.

I smile in reply, wondering if I have seen what I think I have seen – Mark pocketing a shimmering diamond ring.

My heart is pounding with excitement when we finally pull onto the ferry to make our twenty-minute crossing to Vashon. And as we drive through town and across the country roads, all I can think about is if Mark will ask me to marry him this weekend.

I put my hand on Mark's thigh as we make our way down the steep hill that leads to his grandma and grandpa's cabin. At the bottom of the bumpy road, we emerge from the limbs of the overgrown maples to a view of Puget Sound. The cabin is nestled into the hillside with nothing but sand and water out from its front deck. Grandma and Grandpa must have heard our car because they are on the back porch ready to greet us.

Grandpa is a tall slender man and grandma is short with curly gray hair. They look as I imagine grandparents should look.

"We're here!" Mark says and gives me a kiss before he gets out of the car and hugs his grandparents.

"Hi!" I say stepping out of the car, "It's good to see you again."

"It's good to see you too," Grandma says.

I wrap my arms around her. She smells like the ocean.

"Glad you could make it," Grandpa Lowry reaches his hand to mine and pulls me into his chest.

"Thanks," I say, glancing past the beach house to the waves that lap upon the shore, then back to grandpa's smiling eyes. "It's really good to be here."

One by one we file through the front door, which leads to the TV room. The ceiling is low and almost no light makes its way in from the large living room that looks out on the water. The kitchen borders the small TV room, and it is there that we gather for the Vashon Island gossip.

Soon the conversation comes around to me and my family. I tell them about my grandparents from Montana, Honey and Bampa – how Honey likes to fatten me up with homemade orange rolls and apple pie and how I can talk to them about anything from politics to sex while they take my money playing cards. I tell Grandma and Grandpa Lowry that my mom, Honey and Bampa's daughter, was born and raised in

Montana and my dad was born and raised in Austria. My mom was studying voice at the Mozarteum in Salzburg, Austria, when she met my dad and after just six weeks, (a couple weeks less than Mark and I have been together) they were engaged and shortly there after they were married. My brother Putz was born in Austria, a year later. An artist and musician at heart, he is an Army Airborne Ranger who is living in Italy with his wife Loré and will be moving back to Spokane soon.

Grandma and Grandpa ask about my job and I explain that I have been modeling since college, even spent time modeling in Europe, but now, with Mark, I don't see any reason to leave the Northwest. I joke that my college education (BA in Communication, minor in Business) isn't a total waste because I do have to communicate as a model and, since I'm self-employed, I own my own business. As I chat, I glance around the room at the plants and shells that fill every empty space and find myself wondering how Easter cactuses can grow so large, but I don't wonder how I will fit in with Grandma and Grandpa.

"Can you excuse us for a bit?" Mark winks at me then grabs a couple of Budweiser's from the fridge that he had slipped in on our arrival. We walk to the beach, take off our shoes and socks, sit on a rock, and dangle our feet in the water.

"I usually do a few things to help out when I first get here," Mark says, before taking a long swig of beer.

"Sounds good," I say, rubbing my toe gently up and down his shin.

"After we finish our beers, let's go up and see what we can do with that rutted driveway and then chop some firewood."

"Put me to work," I say as we click our cans together in a toast.

We dig trenches on the steep drive to divert rainfall and prune the trees whose branches swept the Prelude earlier. Mark splits wood and I stack logs. Mark wields the ax over his head and cracks it down through each piece of wood with ease. When he stops and turns to me, ax held tight in his right hand, I can't help but feel like a teenager staring at his broad chest as it rises and falls with each breath.

Mark is silent. When I finally look up he takes a deep breath and puffs his chest up more.

"You done?" he laughs and walks closer, "Could you help Grandma with dinner while I finish up here?"

"Sure," I answer and give him a parting kiss.

After dinner, and some Bingo, we say goodnight to Grandma and Grandpa. We retire to the seashell-and-driftwood living room where Mark crawls into an old leather lazy boy and reaches his hand out to mine.

"Come here," he says, pulling me down next to him. The scent of Irish Spring and Budweiser is strong. I swing both legs over Mark's lap.

"I love you," I whisper into his ear, then kiss him gently. "I am so lucky I found you."

"I love you too, Sōn," he says.

I love that he uses my childhood nickname.

Looking around the room, my eyes move from shell to shell in silence. My mind wanders and I imagine myself wearing an ivory dress and looking through a veil into Mark's eyes. I imagine him placing a diamond ring, like the one I hope is in his jacket pocket at this moment, on my ring finger. I close my eyes, nestle my face into his neck and let my mind wander.

There is no engagement ring by the end of our quiet Friday evening together. The following day we spend time with Grandma and Grandpa before venturing into the tiny town of Vashon, walking hand in hand through its small shops. No ring there, either. Saturday evening we enjoy dinner at the cabin with Mark's grandparents, and then gather firewood. On the beach, at the water's edge, we make the perfect fire. We cuddle next to it, each with a drink in hand. When it's time to put out the fire, there is a pile of beer cans, but still no engagement ring. Our pace is slow Sunday afternoon as we stroll the beach, fingers intertwined, and as the sun falls to meet the horizon, I know I've been mistaken. There will be no proposal this weekend. And as darkness creeps across into the sky I find myself wishing on the first star of the night, that I will forget about the ring, and instead simply relish this time together.

Mark is quiet. We stop in front of a wide log buried deep in the sand. Mark sits in the sand, back against the wood, and I sit between his legs, my back resting on his chest. He curls his fingertips around mine and wraps our arms around my waist. He holds me for a long time, then whispers, each word carefully crossing his lips, "I love you, babe. The two of us are going to do so many great things together."

I squeeze my arms tighter and whisper back, "I love you, too." I close my eyes and squeeze him again. "I will love you forever, Mark."

❋

Since meeting Mark, I smile at everyone I pass while on my runs. That is, until today. Today as I run around Green Lake, I'm not smiling. It's a workout, and that is all. I am upset because Mark and I had our first fight.

We had gone crabbing with his dad. We'd started with a cooler of Coors Light and returned to his dad's house in Everett with a cooler of Dungeness crab. We had Crab Louis salads for dinner, topped with Larry's homemade Thousand Island dressing. Mark's mom and Debbie told stories that should have made Mark blush. Mark merely smiled, then added more. Each time he left the table for beer, he gave Debbie, the youngest in the family, a playful nudge, mussing her short sandy hair. When Wendy, the oldest sister spoke, she tucked her dark hair behind her ear then responded with a dimpled smile. Vikki,

26

who was going to be married soon, was the only one of the four kids missing from dinner that night. However, her smile (one that matched Mark's) was everywhere in the family pictures scattered throughout the house. Mark brought me beer. It was cold and went down easy. I watched and knew I wanted to have this, this family closeness. And I wanted to have it with Mark.

As beer and my imagination worked against me on our drive back to Seattle, I began to wonder if Mark wanted to marry me at all, if the Overholts would ever be my family. Mark and I had only seen one another twice in the past week and he seemed emotionally distant. My cheeks were warm and my vision a bit fuzzy. From the passenger seat, I tried to focus on the back of the red Ford truck that was illuminated by our headlights as we began to pass. This is not a good time to ask questions, the evening has been perfect. I reached over and turned down one of Mark's favorite songs by the Doors, "Light My Fire."

"I had an awesome day and I really enjoyed your family," I said, my cheeks growing even warmer. "I would love to spend more time with them. With you, for that matter," I added, looking out the window, this time into darkness.

Mark put his hands at ten and two. They were tight against the steering wheel.

"I've got a lot going on right now," he said.

"I'm trying to understand. I realize you have a new job and your baseball league is starting. But I miss you." I said, looking in his direction, wanting to read his mind.

"We spend most of our free time together." His voice grew louder, "What more do you want?"

"It just seems a waste to be apart, to live apart," I said wishing I could stop myself. "We used to talk about getting married," I continued, tears pouring from my eyes. I wiped them with the back of my hand and went on, "We don't even

27

play basketball together anymore." I sobbed.

"Patience, Sonya," Mark said, having lost his with me.

We drove the rest of the way home in silence.

Slowing to a walk at the end of my run, I sit down on a wooden bench that faces the lake and the Olympic Mountains. The sun penetrates my already-warm body. Tears wait in the corners of my eyes. Why am I in such a hurry now to get married? Mark and I have the rest of our lives together. Leaning into the bench I close my eyes. I have a busy week ahead, a show for Nordstrom, a print job for Lamonts, and a national commercial for Soloflex. I try not to think of the way Mark had seemed distant, preoccupied. I decide I will focus on myself and my work. I will try to be patient.

❊

Pictures are scattered across the carpet. Kneeling, I sort them and choose several to make a prototype of my next composite card for my modeling portfolio. I have a strong fashion shot in a dark suit and two body shots, a black and white lingerie and a running shot, but I need a good close up of my face – a headshot , as it's called in the modeling business. I need to schedule a photo shoot to get the right shot. I pull Vogue from under a Sports Illustrated and begin to search for the look I want, when the phone rings. I press my lips together, wait a beat, set down the magazine, cross the room and pick up the phone.

"Hello."

"Hi!" comes from the other end of the line and my grimace turns to a smile as I walk to the couch and sit down.

"Hi, Mom," I say.

"Is Mark there?"

"No," I answer, my mind spinning. "Why?"

"Well," she begins slowly, "he called your father and…"

She continues after a brief pause, "Well, we thought he must be there."

I know there is only one reason Mark would have called my dad: to ask for my hand in marriage. My mind is now ringing – with wedding bells. I don't hear a thing my mom is saying.

"Mom, can I call you back later?" I ask, ready to say good bye.

"Okay. Good night ," she says.

"Good night," I say, and quickly add, "I love you."

I put my finger to the receiver and push the button down. Smiling, I dial.

"Hi," I say and wait a beat. "I hear you talked to Dad."

"Don't move, I'll be right there," Mark says, slamming down the receiver.

I laugh, imagining the surprised look on his face.

The drive down I-5 normally takes five minutes with no traffic. Mark makes good time, considering he stopped for flowers before zipping past the four exits between our homes, parking his car, and rushing up three flights of stairs to my apartment. It has been just eight minutes when I open the door to a colorful bouquet and the sweet smell of his leather bomber jacket.

Mark wraps his arms around me and gives me a long kiss before he closes the door behind us. He lays the flowers on a side table, sits me down on the closest chair, holds my left hand, and kneels in front of me. One by one, tears run down my cheeks as the notes of "Unforgettable" melt into the background. Holding a piece of paper in his other hand, Mark looks me in the eye and begins to recite a poem.

ONE is for our bright future to come.
TWO is because I know that I truly love you.
THREE is for the happiness that you bring to me.

FOUR is because my life feels more complete than before.
FIVE is for the way your love makes me feel so alive.
SIX is for when I close my eyes, forever your beautiful smile sticks.
SEVEN is for what we've created…our own special heaven.
EIGHT is because when …

"I haven't quite figured this line out yet," he apologizes, and glances at his hand-written notes before he continues.

NINE is for you being mine.
TEN is because all that we do I can't wait to do again.
ELEVEN is to multiply what I said in seven.
TWELVE is for all that you are, the joy you bring each day,
—and because I love you more than words can say.

He lets his notes drop to the floor.

"Sonya, will you marry me?" he asks, reaching a hand into his jacket pocket. "Will you spend the rest of your life with me?"

I bend to kiss him and whisper, "Yes."

Our lips touch and onto my finger he slips a gold band with a single diamond. I close my eyes and wrap my arms around him, "Yes, Mark, yes."

Mark explains that he's been carrying the wedding ring in his jacket pocket for a month. He brought it with him to Vashon, but had been waiting to propose to me next week on the evening of his sister's wedding, where he planned to give me the ring and recite the poem overlooking the Puget Sound. He would have worn a tux and would have handed me a rose for each stanza. It would have been romantic, but tonight and forevermore, with a bouquet of flowers from Safeway and wearing blue jeans and a UW t-shirt, Mark Overholt captures my heart.

TOGETHER FOREVER

Sitting side by side at our kitchen table, Mark finishes paperwork on an insurance claim while I admire the paintings in our new apartment. Two weeks ago we interviewed for the apartment management position at College Street Apartments in West Seattle. We got the job, and five days later moved in together. Though the small one-bedroom apartment has no real charm of its own, it made a metamorphosis as we blended our styles, eclectic and classic bachelor, to make it our home. Mark also suggested we paint – but not the walls. Instead, that October day we drove to Northwest Art & Frame and bought several large canvases and an array of bright acrylic paints. We spent the entire afternoon mixing vibrant colors on canvas. Each with paintbrushes in hand, we stood in the living room, staring at the large white spaces that were placed on our new easel. Then working as a team, we brought the canvases to life, one at a time, while sipping on glasses of Chardonnay and laughing at the bad Karaoke that made its way from the neighborhood tavern through our open window. When we hung the art work on our walls, we truly felt the place was ours. I can't help but smile now looking at the bright, almost-childlike painting we chose to hang above the couch.

Finally I look down at the box that sits in front of me on the table and the warmth I was feeling drains from my body. Inside the box is the one thing that still needs to be done to make the wedding plans come together – the invitations. Three hundred invitations that need to be addressed, stuffed, and sent. Overwhelmed, I tap my new black calligraphy pen on the glass, take a deep breath, and pull out one ivory envelope.

"I hate stuff like this," I complain as I open my tattered address book. "Do you write Mr. & Mrs.? What if they use different last names? I don't even want to start." The blank envelope under my pen stares back at me.

"Here, give me those," Mark laughs and grabs a pile of envelopes. "I'll do my family and friends and you do yours."

"Thanks," I say.

I work on the Gaubinger list and Mark on the Overholt list. With each pen stroke I think of all that has happened since Mark asked me to marry him nearly six months ago. The decision to marry Mark was easy for me. I love him with all my heart. And Mom was elated of course; but it was not the same for Dad. Dad made no mention of my engagement to his employees at the shop or to any of his friends. He was getting used to the idea of losing his daughter, in his own time. It wasn't until Dad and I met for our weekly Tuesday picnic lunch in Seattle (when he's in town picking up food and wine for the shop) that we had an opportunity to talk face to face, and I had the opportunity to convince him that Mark was the right man for me. Dad could see it in my eyes: I was in love. And once he knew that, he opened to the idea of my engagement and opened his heart to Mark. He was ready to help with the wedding.

"Why do you want to get married in Seattle and not Spokane?" my parents had asked.

"Seattle is my home now," I had explained.

That was all they needed; with their full support, the

planning began. My dad, though not a practicing Catholic, is Catholic, and my mom is Methodist. Instead of going to separate churches while I was growing up, our family spent Sundays hiking, sledding, walking, and playing together. Sundays were family days. I consider myself simply spiritual, and since Mark is Catholic, a short Catholic wedding was the answer.

Planning for this wedding, this new life together, hasn't been easy. We asked Father Doug, a priest who knows Mark's family, to perform the ceremony and then reserved the church for the evening of November 8. Between basketball games and photo shoots, I've chosen a wedding photographer, decided on a florist, and hired Hillary, a friend from high school, to sing during the first part of our reception until the DJ and dancing begin. I've worked out the reception details, including the banquet permit, the linen rentals, and the decorations. Finding a reception hall within our criteria was a challenge: a location not far from the church at reasonable price that allowed outside catering. But after researching what seemed like a hundred places, calling, driving, and begging, I found the perfect spot, the Ballard Elks Lodge in Shilshole.

As the bride, I have done most of the planning but Mark has had a few responsibilities. One has been to make sure all the groomsmen got fitted for their tuxes. Not an easy task. I have hounded Mark, who has hounded his groomsmen and ushers, and now Micky, Mark's best man; Chris, Dave, Joe, Mike, the groomsmen; and Jeff and Paul, the ushers, have all been fitted. Mark has wrapped their gifts – Bavarian beer steins from Dad's shop – and all that is left on his to-do list is to get his passport for our honeymoon trip to Greece.

We have registered at The Bon Marché together. Blue Pinstripe Lenox is our casual china pattern, and against my better judgment and with pressure from Mark's mom, we have registered for formal china, Lenox Federal Gold. We have registered for the regulars: flatware, stemware, barware, serve ware, cutlery, linens, home decor, and more. But both of us are excited about our extras. If our friends and family look far enough down our list, under miscellaneous, they will find mountain bikes and of course basketball shoes (Nike high-tops – men's sizes 6 ½ and 9 ½.)

My wedding dress is not what I had first envisioned. I had planned to wear an elegant sheath dress, like my mom wore in her wedding. In fact, I had hoped to wear her dress, but since I find breathing essential, my mom's wedding dress with its tiny waist was out of the question. Instead mom and I have scoured the bridal shops of Seattle where we came away empty-handed until a recommendation led us 20 miles north to Zola's Bridal shop. It was there I found my dress. No frills. Simple and affordable (I wasn't going to spend thousands of my parent's dollars on a wedding dress.) My dress is white satin with the sheen of silk and the ideal fit for my boyishly straight body. Its full skirt gives the illusion of a small waist and its lightly adorned bodice with a plunging, off the shoulder neckline places an emphasis on my bust and face. The last fitting is etched in my mind.

With my hair pulled back in a tight ponytail and no makeup, I gazed into the three-way mirror and admired my dress from every angle. The dress fit perfectly. I ran my hands gently down the bodice of the dress. I could imagine Mark doing the same.

"You look stunning," my mom said, leaning back in her chair.

She was smiling. She was enjoying her own vision of me in my wedding dress, perhaps walking down the aisle on Dad's arm; ready to be given away to the man I love. Something I too could see, as if it were real.

Mark will be wearing his black tuxedo with tails. When he

first tried it on at the tux shop, he left me breathless and eager to see him at the end of the aisle surrounded by his groomsmen and my bridesmaids in their classic black satin dresses holding bouquets bursting with Sonia roses. Standing in my wedding dress, I could imagine them all waiting for me to walk down the aisle. Like a fashion show, the church pews adorned with ribbons and roses will lead me down the runway to Mark and our new life as husband and wife.

We are ready for our wedding day. It has been stressful at times, but we've made it through the tough stuff and by the time I start thinking about the four-tiered wedding cake with buttercream frosting, we have finished addressing the invitations. What alone had seemed an overwhelming task was easy when we worked as a team. Our Catholic wedding counselor talked to us in one of our sessions about working together after I had complained about the struggles we were having due to our busy schedules. She reminded us that a marriage is a team effort. We had agreed. "I have one more baseball tournament," Mark had said, "and then we'll have more time. We'll have the rest of our lives together."

I look at the canvas above the couch. I look through the bright colors we have splashed upon its surface and see a man and a woman holding one another. I look at the overflowing box of invitations and envelopes. And then I take a final look at the crisp white invitation with delicate Parchment style text, before I tuck it into the newly addressed envelope. I know Mark and I can work as a team and I look forward to our future.

Mr. and Mrs. Werner Gaubinger
Request the honour of your presence
At the marriage of their daughter
Sonya
To

Mark Alan Overholt
On Friday, the eighth of November
Nineteen hundred and ninety-one
At half past seven o'clock
St. John Catholic Church
121 North Eightieth Street
Seattle, Washington

❈

Two weeks before our wedding we drive to Spokane for my last bridal shower. We pack up Mark's company car, a red Chevy Lumina, with our bags and his files, because he has work to do there, as well. We will be staying with my parents, and I am especially pleased that they will have the opportunity to get to know Mark better. He will also be able to meet my brother before the wedding. Putz and his wife Loré have just returned from Italy.

Saturday morning after breakfast my dad works at the deli, Mark sets up his papers and insurance claims, and Mom and I drive to my bridal shower given by Carol, the mother of my bridesmaid, Leslie Emmons. Oddly, none of my bridesmaids is at the shower. I will not even see them until the rehearsal dinner, and of course, the wedding. Except for Tami-su, they all live far away. Kirsten, my maid of honor, works at a production company in New York; Lillie just moved to Chicago; Leslie works for an attorney in Washington, D.C., and Kris lives in Hawaii where she works as a profusionist (she regulates patients' blood during heart surgery.) Even without my bridesmaids here, I feel loved and celebrated.

Before dinner, Mark and I and my parents stroll through the neighborhood where I grew up, laughing, talking, and taking pictures. Mark and I pose, arms around each other, in front of my parents' 70s rambler, smiling, eager, and in love. We return to the house where my father pours four glasses of

Cabernet, and we all raise them for a toast. "To Mark and Sonya," my dad says, "to their wedding and their future together."

Mark slips his hand into mine and squeezes.

On Sunday, with all the gifts and cards from the bridal shower packed in the Lumina, Mark and I head for Seattle. Even though this has been a wonderful weekend, we are looking forward to being alone, away from parents and friends and well-wishers. As we drive west on I-90 on this warm, fall day, I relax into the passenger seat and watch out the window as the golden grass of eastern Washington blows about in the wind. When I hear the click of the turn signal I look at Mark and find a mischievous smile in his eyes.

We take the next exit and search for a place to stop. The hills are few and gentle, and sagebrush lines the expanse of open fields. We could be in Kansas. Were it not for a tall haystack and the shelter of two gnarled trees that call to us, we might turn back to the freeway. Instead we follow Snyder Road across railroad tracks and down a narrow dirt road where we pull in amongst the hay and sun-drenched branches.

Mark leans to me for a kiss and we barely touch our lips together when he turns away and opens his door to get out. By the time I hop out of my seat, Mark has come to meet me, and with his warm body, he backs me firmly against the side of the car and slips my Levis down my hips before unbuttoning his shorts. As his body pushes against mine, the heat of the metal door heightens the sensation of his touch. He reaches up, holds my face in both hands, and kisses me hard. With the midday sun burning down on us, I hold him tight. I breathe him, taste him, and love him with all my heart. He pushes my back hard into the car and I close my eyes and love him loving me.

Fresh air surrounds our bodies and our hearts pound as we relax against the door. Still breathing hard, I open my eyes and find Mark's lazy smile looking back at mine. We hold one another for a long while before getting back into the car. As we are about to leave, Mark reaches behind the seat and pulls out a card. "I meant to give this to you earlier this weekend, but right now seems to be the perfect time."

The card reads:

I've looked at you so many times
To see your happy smile,
I've come to you for company
To talk a little while,
I've laughed with you and shared with you
A world of special things—
I've learned from you the precious joys
That only caring brings.

It is followed by Mark's personal sentiment:

Sonya,

Until the day I die, I will try my best to make each day special for you. Just having you in my life makes each day one to look forward to.

Forever in Love,
Mark

I close the card and run my finger over the dimple that widens his broad smile. It deepens with my touch. How can I be so lucky? We kiss again; his lips are soft against mine and I can feel his breath on my cheek as he moves to kiss my neck. He runs his fingers through my long hair, and holding the back of my neck, rests his lips on my forehead.

"God, I love you," he says.

Mark takes a deep breath, gives me one last kiss, and starts the car. He rolls down his window, and then circles the car around to drive towards the freeway. I hear the rustling of paper in the back and turn to see cards from my bridal shower spread across the seat, blowing in the wind. I look through the back window and watch as the dust that had softly swirled around our feet with our earlier footsteps forms a low cloud that trails behind us as we near the railroad tracks. I glance once more at Mark, then reach back to straighten the cards.

PART II – LOST DAYS
October 20th, 1991 - Spokane, Washington

IMPACT

A train engine hits our car. As I'm being catapulted through the back window of our Chevy Lumina, my dad is at home in Spokane raking the dried needles that have fallen from Ponderosa Pine in the yard. The air is crisp and sweet and the sun, still high in the sky, beats down on him. He straightens up slowly and soaks in the golden hues that fill the landscape he has tended for seventeen years. Inside our house, my mom stands at the sink and washes dishes. A hint of a smile crosses her lips and she smoothes back her short dark hair as she watches dad through the window. She imagines how handsome he will look walking me down the aisle in his black smoking jacket, the one he was wearing when they married twenty-eight years ago.

The ring of the phone interrupts her thoughts. Mom dries her hands and crosses the kitchen floor. "Hello. Gaubinger residence," she answers, as she has for all her married years.

"Carole Gaubinger?" an unfamiliar voice asks.

"Yes."

"Do you have a daughter named Sonya?"

"Yes," she answers after a long silence. A tightness creeps into her chest.

"This is Dr. Anderson. I'm calling from Ritzville Hospital. Your daughter has been in an accident."

There is silence and her hands begin to tremble.

"Ma'am? Are you there?"

"Yes," mom sputters.

"I'm very sorry." The voice keeps coming. "Ma'am, you'll want to go to Deaconess Hospital in Spokane," he says. "Sonya is being flown there by Lifebird, please drive carefully." Enunciating each word slowly and clearly, he adds, "Please do not speed."

"What happened?" she asks.

"Your daughter is badly hurt," he says. "The car she was in was hit by a train."

My mom crumples to the floor. The phone, hanging from its cord, swings side to side. How can this be happening? Sonya and Mark were just here a couple hours ago. They…they…

She rises to her knees and scrambles to catch the phone. "Are you there?" she asks, short of breath, heart racing.

"Yes ma'am, I'm here."

"What about Mark?" she begs. "Do you know anything about Mark?"

"Only your daughter is being flown to Deaconess, ma'am."

"Werner," mom screams and is still screaming when dad bursts into the kitchen.

My parents speed to the hospital. They move through the hospital corridors swiftly, their minds numb to the living nightmare. Once at the ER they're ushered into an isolated waiting room. The chairs are stiff. Plastic plants accompany rumpled magazines on the side tables. There's a photograph of the sun setting across a lake; the water is flat, calm. My parents wait. No doctors speak to them. When they ask questions, no one has answers.

My parents call their friend Donald, a doctor who works

with high-risk pregnancies. Dr. Donald Barford comes to the hospital. He's able to get a few answers, but what little information is gathered is not good. I am in critical condition, and am being stabilized and prepped for surgery. When a chaplain enters the room, my parents realize my life is hanging in the balance and it's time to call family.

Mom is talking to her sister when a nurse enters the waiting room. Mom sets down the phone with a trembling hand.

"Carole?" the nurse begins with a soft voice. Mom stands and is followed by dad. "Werner," the nurse continues, "Sonya is about to go into surgery. She won't be able to talk to you, but you can see her now. Follow me."

My parents look to one another for reassurance. Three hours have passed since they received the call that changed all of our lives. They follow the nurse's long dark ponytail down the hall to room 4, Deaconess Hospital.

The nurse brings my parents in to see me. Sonya? This is not their Sonya. The body, my body, lies before them. It is large and swollen. My eyes, and all identity, are hidden deep in my bruised and swollen skin. Wild blonde hair spun with blood and weeds encircles my face. Tubes are taped to needles protruding from my arms and legs. A nurse begins to clean the opening where a large white tube enters my chest. The tube is attached to one of many noisy machines.

Dad weaves on his feet, nauseated. Mom speaks softly, telling me that they love me, but the only answers come from the buzzing machines. My body is lifeless, in a silent struggle to survive.

They both hold my hand.

"We have to take her to surgery now," says the nurse, "We'll look for you in the waiting room when the surgery is over."

My brother enters the small waiting room. He's dressed in black shorts and a black t-shirt and tall black boots that reach his knees. He's got a crew cut. His towering frame crosses the room in two strides and he puts his arms around mom.

"Oh Putz, I'm so glad you're here."

"Have you heard anything?" he asks. He's afraid. He can't imagine a world without me. The army prepared him for a lot of things, but not for the loss of his little sister, his Sōn.

"She just went into surgery." Dad answers.

Six long hours pass. Finally a nurse enters the room and explains that I'm being moved to ICU.

"Can we see her?" mom asks.

"Soon, Dr. Perry would like to talk to you first."

"How's she doing?" mom searches for more.

"The surgery went well. The bones needed to be set right away."

"But will she be okay?" dad questions.

"Well, it's still early, but what's important now is that Sonya made it through the surgery. Dr. Perry can tell you more about that."

"I'll wait here and call Honey and Bampa," mom says, "you two go."

The nurse motions Dad and Putz to follow her down another long white hall. They enter a small room where they meet a tall man with dark curly hair standing near the edge of a counter. His eyes sparkle like he has just won a national championship.

"Hi, I'm Dr. Perry," he says, his voice pumping with adrenaline, "the surgery went very well. Sonya is on her way to the ICU, you should be able to see her soon." He lifts several x-rays and places them on a lighted board. "As you can see from the x-ray, Sonya's leg was badly broken and her arm has what is called a comminuted fracture. We were able to put a rod in the femur with no trouble," he explains, stepping from behind the counter and pointing to the x-ray on the far side of the lighted board. It shows the upper part of a leg, my leg, with a rod running the length of the bone, inside the bone. The rod looks to be held in place by two screws that protrude out the side of the bone.

Dad and Putz look on in silence. Putz's eyes leave the x-ray then follow Dr. Perry's arm down the side of his scrubs. His eyes stop when they reach the floor. Dr. Perry is covered in blood from his knees down. Putz's tall body begins to sway. He closes his eyes. When he opens them, he focuses on the x-ray.

"The arm was shattered. I lined it up as best I could and got the screw to hold." He explains, beaming.

Dad studies the x-ray – studies the shattered right arm that used to be my shooting arm.

"It's kind of crooked."

Dr. Perry purses his lips then points at the x-ray again, "The small fragments should absorb into the body." He glances at a huge chunk of bone just above where the bicep would be. "Others will either attach to the bone or remain suspended in the tissue."

"Thank you, doctor."

An hour later, my parents follow another nurse to my room in the Intensive Care Unit. People are allowed to enter the room only two at a time, so Putz waits. The nurse explains that I'm stable for now, that I have a bruised heart, and a lacerated spleen and kidney, and will have constant monitoring and care in the ICU. He doesn't tell them about the separated sternum, cracked ribs, internal bleeding, and concussion, nor that I could develop an embolism that could kill me at any time.

"Sonya, we're right here," mom and dad say. "We love you." mom gently presses my hand.

I open my swollen eyes briefly, and then with great difficulty, ask, "Where's Mark?"

I gasp, trying to be heard over the noisy machines. My

mind, battling pain and drugs, focuses on one thing, Mark. I don't know where I am, or what's going on. I try again: "Tell me, please, is Mark okay?"

"You're going to be okay," Mom answers, squeezing my hand.

I close my eyes.

"Where is Mark?" I gasp.

"It's going to be okay," Dad says. "You're going to be okay."

Uncontrolled tears escape, mixing with blood on the gurney. "Where is Mark?" I ask.

Beeping echoes through the room.

Mom looks to Dad.

"Tell her," he whispers.

"I'm so sorry." Mom leans closer. "You've been in an accident. You've been badly hurt."

"What about Mark?" I cry, my body now shaking.

"Hush, Sonya. Hush."

"Where is Mark?" I gasp.

"You've been in an accident," mom repeats. "A terrible accident. You are going to be okay, Sonya, but I'm so sorry, honey, Mark didn't make it. Mark is dead."

Days later an article hits the sports page in the Spokesman Review.

GAUBINGER IN INTENSIVE CARE

Sonya Gaubinger, former University High School and Eastern Washington University basketball player, remains in intensive care at Deaconess Medical Center with injuries sustained Sunday in a car-train accident near Ritzville.

Gaubinger, 25, was a passenger in a car driven by

her fiancé, Mark Overholt, that was struck by a Burlington Northern train at a crossing on Snyder Road. She was thrown through the rear window and suffered multiple fractures and a punctured lung. She underwent six hours of surgery on Sunday.

Overholt, 25, died from internal injures at the site of the crash.

HOLDING ON

The mind is a powerful thing and it took care of me in the first moments following the accident, leaving all that happened buried in the depth of my unconscious mind. Only police records were left to piece together what happened that Sunday when the Burlington Northern freight train glided along the tracks and disturbed the silence, whipping sagebrush and grass with its passing. Traveling sixty-five miles an hour the train tried to stop but couldn't as it bore down on our red Chevy Lumina. Steel wheels screeched on the tracks, and then tossed our car high in the air. As the train came to a stop nearly a mile from the accident site, it swept more sagebrush and grass, and swept away the hopes and dreams of those who had been in its path.

The engine crew must have wondered why our car had crossed the tracks that beautiful fall day. Had they known that we had just made love, would their horror have been even greater? Could it have been any greater than what they must have felt at impact or when they heard my faint cry in the distance as one man leapt down from the locomotive?

According to police records, our car had just crossed the tracks when the engine hit the driver's side of the vehicle. Like a tattered rag doll, I was thrown from the car. I flew through the air and fell strewn across the rocks. My limbs lay askew, bent at unthinkable angles, covered in dirt and blood, open to the world ever so briefly before the Lumina came crashing down upon me, somehow leaving me untouched.

The young man who heard my faint cry had jumped from the train and landed on the jagged black rocks that lined the rails then looked back to where he had just witnessed the full force of driving steel. His heart must have skipped a beat before he followed the tracks that lead to dust and devastation.

"Help!" came my faint cry.

The man moved faster, his heart pounding. There came another cry, this one louder than before. The man's breath must have been cut short as he began to lope through the high grass and tumbleweeds, and ran to reach my calls for help. When he found our car, which had been crushed and tossed by the train, it was lying over me. Somehow I lay untouched beneath it. Blood and dirt covered my body and face. I screamed as he tried to comfort me.

Officer Ditmer was the first officer to arrive on the scene at 2:30 in the afternoon. Broken glass was everywhere. Broken crystal, broken china and two suitcases worth of clothing were scattered on impact. Officer Mittman was the next to arrive. He reached inside the car and checked Mark's pulse. Mark's body had been thrown to the passenger side of the vehicle; his feet were still planted on the driver's side underneath the brake pedal. Mark had no pulse and was not breathing.

Officer Ditmer called for Lifebird and surveyed my injuries (possible extreme dislocation of the right shoulder and internal injuries) then kept me warm with a blanket from the train. Officer Ditmer spoke with me to help keep me conscious, knowing the statistics, knowing that a person who remains conscious after trauma has an increased chance of survival.

What did Officer Ditmer and I talk about? Did he ask my name? Could I answer him? Did I ask about Mark? Did he answer me?

It took eight minutes for an ambulance to arrive from Ritzville. I was transported to the hospital in Ritzville and the Lifebird helicopter touched down soon after and swept me away. It landed on the rooftop of Deaconess Hospital at 3:14. I was pulled from the coffin-like chamber of Lifebird. Wind from the slowing propellers whipped my hair and the sound deadened my fading screams as they lowered me to the gurney and whisked me toward the waiting doors of surgery and my unknown fate.

The doctors forced a chest tube between my ribs to repair a punctured lung then stabilized me as best they could. I was transferred to a fracture table for surgery. A six-inch incision was made from hip to mid thigh. Using a metal rod and Recon Nail, the doctor pulled my fractured femur into place, and brought my right leg back together.

Next, I was transferred to a C-arm table where a three-inch deltoid splitting incision was made on my right shoulder. My bursa was removed before the surgeon cut into the rotator cuff. He worked to stabilize my shattered right arm, using a Siedel Nail (a rod with a screw locking mechanism), to bring my right arm back into place. There was a blood transfusion. Last they cleaned and stitched a five-inch laceration on my head, where I broke through the car window.

I suffered a broken right thigh bone, a shattered right arm, a punctured lung, bruised heart, lacerated spleen and kidney, chipped vertebrae, separated sternum, cracked ribs, internal bleeding, concussion, skull laceration, and numerous cuts and abrasions. The most serious of the injuries were the fractures that allowed bone marrow to enter my body and bloodstream.

Loose bone marrow not only adds to the ongoing threat of infection but can in itself cause an embolism, and death.

❋

My parents and brother focus on life. Sonya is alive. For now that is all they have. They can't look to the future because my future is unknown except for the fact that it does not include Mark.

My Aunt Cathy, mom's younger sister, drives Honey and Bampa three and a half hours from their home in Missoula and they arrive in Spokane the next day. Cathy looks like my mom, with a touch of grey in her hair and narrow red-framed glasses that rest low on her nose. Cathy takes charge. She is a rock, where a rock is needed, giving stability to my family that now has to eat, work, sleep, and maintain lives within a new reality.

My family spends the next six days in a rotating vigil. Honey and Bampa come to the hospital and wait. Bampa stands for hours with his hands deep in the pockets of his camel slacks, his lemon yellow U of M sweater soft across his shoulders as he leans toward the door each time a nurse enters the waiting room in hopes of news of his granddaughter's fate. Honey sits alongside Mom. They speak, quietly, glancing frequently at the door. Bringing warmth to the room, Honey looks dressed for a bridge game or perhaps a luncheon, her turquoise slacks with matching blouse accenting her pale skin and soft pink lips. But the warmth cannot mask her worry and fear.

Only family members, two at a time, are allowed to enter the ICU room for five minutes each hour. The ICU room is a contained world that spans the gap between life and death. A twenty-four hour fluorescent day. The health professionals' constant prodding, poking, and monitoring don't allow for sleep. For me, nightmare and reality coexist.

Morphine seduces my mind. I open my eyes hoping to see

Mark. "Mark?" I call. A nurse gently reminds me that Mark is dead.

The room buzzes.

Time passes. My eyes open.

"I need to call Kirsten." I whisper.

My eyes close.

"I need to call Kirsten," I repeat, perhaps because I feel that Kirsten, my maid of honor, needs to be told that I'm in the hospital. Kirsten, of course, already knows.

"Good morning." The nurse steps closer and gently touches my forehead.

"What time is it?" I ask. Blinking, I see two images of the nurse with the long blonde hair, the same nurse who spent three hours carefully cleaning my hair of debris. Saving my hair, rather than shaving my head when the doctor put forty-three stitches across my scalp.

"3:30 a.m." The nurse raises her eyebrows. "So it's too early to be making a phone call."

"That means its 6:30 in New York and Kirsten will just be leaving for work."

The nurse nods her head and smiles, guessing that I must have escaped the collision with minimal brain damage.

The nurse dials the phone. The conversation is short. Kirsten calls Leslie. They know I will survive.

My family is one of many that sit and pace the ICU waiting room, praying for a miracle in a place where the odds are against them.

I improve and after a week in the hospital my family receives word that I will be leaving ICU. They are overwhelmed with emotion – with happiness, because I will survive; with fear wondering how I will go on with my life; and with guilt for being one of the few families that will not be leaving the

ICU to plan a funeral.

Searching through stacks of magazines and newspaper s in the waiting room for something to occupy his mind, Bampa runs across an article in the newspaper about my accident. He reads stoically, trying to imagine the world that existed less than a week ago. He tries to imagine how I will find the courage to live, now. He glances to the seats next to him. Honey is sitting with Mom. Both have barely slept over the last week and their eyes are weary. They, of course, have read the article but Bampa folds the paper and slips it under a stack of magazines. Once is enough.

A hospital counselor arrives and speaks to my family. The counselor asks questions. She learns that mom is from Montana and asks her about her home town. My parents don't care to talk about Montana, they're worried about me. They choose not to see the counselor again. A man from the insurers of Mark's company car arrives with papers to sign. "Don't worry," he says, "we'll pay for everything." My parents can only think about me. They don't sign the papers. My parents never see him again. Burlington Northern railroad calls asking questions. Mom and Dad have no answers. They can only think about one thing. Will I survive? And if I do, will I be the same Sonya?

PART III
October 27th, 1991 - Spokane, Washington

AWAKENING

I open my eyes slowly. It's bright. My eyelids are heavy. My eyes shut. I open them again. Everything is fuzzy. I lift my eyebrows high trying to keep my eyes open. I blink and work to focus and as I look around the room I wonder for a moment if it has all been a dream. Each breath takes more effort than it should and sharp pains radiate through my body. The small table on my left is loaded with flowers, evidence that this is not a dream. I blink more, trying to better focus my eyes, focus my mind. The room is small, there is a TV anchored to the far wall. Buzzing and beeping sounds linger, but beyond that there is silence. I grab the metal rail to my left and turn my head to the side. There is a woman sitting by the window.

"Mom?"

"Yes, Sonya," my mom answers, turning in her chair in time to see my eyes slowly close then open again. I see two of everything and my left eyelid droops across the pupil making it more difficult to see.

"Mom?"

"Yes," she says, then leans closer, "I'm right here."

"Was there a funeral already?"

"Yes," she finds the control to the hospital bed, and raises my head so I can see her without straining my neck. "They had Mark's funeral while you were in Intensive Care."

A single tear rolls down my cheek. I have no reply.

After the accident I spent days drifting in and out of a morphine induced slumber where dreams, hopes, and reality touched my mind and left me guessing. Now it's as if I've finally woken up. When I left the ICU, morphine was replaced with the pain killer Percocet, and though I'm still doped, a cloud has lifted from my mind and I'm aware of what is going on around me. I "wake up" in room 12 knowing that Mark is dead. I don't know how I know; I just know.

One week earlier Mark and I had played what became our last basketball game together. After the game I had teased him about getting love handles. I had grabbed what was mostly skin sitting on the bones above his pale blue Nike shorts and smiled. His eyes had drained.

"I'm kidding." I'd said, drawing my moist body close.

Mark hadn't smiled.

"I'm sorry," I'd said as I stepped back.

The corners of his lips had moved slightly and I gave him a kiss, and another and another.

I can almost feel Mark's lips against mine now as I close my heavy eyelids and fall to sleep, thankful Mark had accepted my apology.

My eyelids lift slowly then drop down tight again and again from the sheer weight of them. As the haze clears once more, I'm aware of a form moving on the television screen. Motions set to familiar music. A graceful presentation of body and strength. I struggle to open my eyes more fully and strain to focus. The blurred woman in the hot pink looks familiar. She has a lean body and toned muscles that move with ease and long blond hair. As my vision clears, my groggy mind makes the connection. I'm watching myself in my first national commercial. With my broken body throbbing in pain, I stare in disbelief at the picture perfect ghost from my past. I close my eyes and allow the pain to permeate my body.

Family and friends take turns at my bedside, a few make the four and a half hour trip from Seattle. They all bring flowers and listening ears that I fill with stories of Mark. I do my best to be strong. The painkillers and my profession as a model take over and I always manage a smile. But when they leave, I'm spent. Most of my visitors are forgotten. My thoughts are occupied by memories of Mark that play like movies in my mind.

Mark's heart beats against my back as I lean into him. We sit on the roof-top of my apartment, bottle in hand. I touch my champagne flute to my lips, and look into the star filled sky.

"What an awesome surprise," I say, melting into his body.

"I'm glad you traded shifts at work," he says, champagne mingling with each word.

"Me too," I say, drinking in the view. "I just wish it were that simple for Vikki's wedding next week." I take another sip. "I really want to be at the rehearsal dinner with you."

"I know," Mark says, kissing my cheek. "At least you'll be able to make the wedding and the reception."

Mark had understood that filming the national Soloflex commercial might be a big break in my career, but it hadn't seemed that important to me; what had been important was for us to be together.

I want to be alone in my hospital room. But when I am, I can't bear it. I look at the growing collection of flowers and feel a burning in my chest. I don't want these damn flowers. I want Mark. I want our life back. My body is always in pain, but I can only feel the pain in my heart.

When I run out of tears, I stare at the TV.

"How are you doing?" Dad asks, walking through the door with Putz by his side.

"Okay," I answer.

"I spoke to Larry and Joan," he says, pulling a chair close to the bed.

I don't answer, just close my eyes.

"They're coming to see you this weekend."

"Good," I manage. Opening my eyes, I look at the sheet that lay across my lap. What will I say to them? If I had never met Mark, their son would still be alive.

"You okay?" my dad asks, cupping my shoulder with his strong hand.

"Yeah," I look up. "Yes, that'll be good."

My brother jumps in. "How are you feeling?" he says, sitting in a chair set against the nearest wall. "Mom said your leg's getting better."

"I guess," I shrug my good shoulder. "It still hurts like hell."

Putz smiles. "Of course it does," he says, and scoots his chair closer. "You're tough, Sōn. You'll get through this."

A tear forms, but I hold it back. The three of us talk for awhile until Putz stands.

"Gotta go," he says and gives me a kiss on the forehead. "Time to get back to work."

"See you, Putz," I say to his broad back as he steps out the door. I lie still for a moment then turn to Dad.

"How's everything at the shop?" I ask.

"Good, but when Mom gets here I have to get back," Dad says, more to himself than to me. He asks if there is anything I need. There is, but Dad can't get it for me. No one can.

Mom walks in. Dad gives her a hug, gives me a kiss, and leaves for work.

"Mom?" I ask, "have you talked to Brice?"

"No," she says, her eyes squinting, sifting through the murk known as the recent past. "I don't think I called him. I don't even know his last name."

Brice and I met when I first moved to Seattle. Both basketball fanatics, we spent time together on and off the court, but my parents had no idea how to reach him.

I recite the number for mom. She dials and hands me the receiver.

"Hi, Brice," I say, my voice tentative and weak.

"Sonya," he answers. I imagine his warm smile on the other end of the line, "It's been too long."

"Yeah," I agree. After meeting Mark, I had been busy.

"How you doin'?" he asks.

"Well," I answer, unsure of how to respond, "not real good."

"Everything okay with you and Mark?" he asks. "I'm sorry I didn't RSVP. I'm not going to be able to make it to your wedding."

"Brice," I say, "there isn't going to be a wedding."

"Why not?"

I take a deep breath.

"We got hit by a train." I take another breath and look at my mom's hand as it gently reaches to mine.

"Right." He laughs and then sings with a twang in his voice, "Sonya gets hit by a train. Sounds like a country song." He laughs again.

"Really, Brice," I say, "Mark and I were hit by a train and Mark was killed."

"You're kidding, right?" he asks, his voice now urgent.

"No," I say, swallowing hard, "I'm not."

I can't imagine telling the story again, but realize I will be telling it the rest of my life.

Honey and Bampa spend hours by my side. Much of the time is spent in silence, but they are there, keeping me alive with their presence.

"Let me get a picture with you and Bampa." My mom leans over the end of the bed rail and snaps a shot of Bampa and me. I have a scraggly braid tied with a pale blue ribbon, thanks to the caring nurse who saved me from the razor, and a black eye. I lean into Bampa and smile. The shot should have included Mark. It should have been taken at our wedding, celebrating our commitment to one another and our families. Then I would have had a reason to smile. Still, as my mom snaps the shutter, the one and only time during my stay in the hospital, she freezes that moment in time with a smile.

Bampa sits down long enough to rest his hand on Honey's leg and pick up his book.

"I think it's time we go and give Sonya a chance to rest," he says, tapping his hand on Honey's pale pink slacks.

She stands up slowly and comes to the side of my bed.

"Can we get you anything before we go?" she asks, knowing my reply.

"No, I'm fine," I answer.

"We love you," she says, gray waves of hair softly framing her wide eyes while the corners of her mouth work to form a smile. I sense the fear in her words. Not fear that I won't survive, but perhaps that I have. A fear of losing her only granddaughter to what could be a fate worse than death; a lifetime of grieving. Death has become a part of her life as her friends, one by one, have become widows and widowers. She has witnessed first hand a widow's suffering. And now she worries that I too will be eaten up by sorrow.

"We'll be back in the morning." She leans forward and gives me a kiss, reaching with both hands to hold my good hand tight. "Okay?" she asks, with a final squeeze.

"Okay," I answer, taking in the scent of her warm cheek and feeling the comfort I knew as a young child in her arms.

Mom, who has been looking out the window, comes alive and walks Honey and Bampa out. I am glad to be alone. I close my eyes. My chest aches, each side rises and falls to a separate rhythm as the ribs try to reattach to the sternum. My chest tube has been removed, but where the ribs were pried apart there is a stabbing pain. My arm is strapped to my body and throbs just enough to deaden the pain in my back and leg. When the day nurse walks in, I open my eyes and struggle to bring her into focus. She sets down a small paper cup with tiny folds filled with Percocet and another filled with water. I take them without hesitation.

One night earlier, I had asked the nurse to wake me up at 4 a.m. for painkillers. Instead I awoke in tears at 5:30 a.m. Thankful that I haven't been forgotten today, I down the Percocet, then hand the nurse the short paper cup and ask for more water.

"That's good, drink plenty of water." She looks at me, pleased. "In fact, later today I'd like to get you out of bed to use the bathroom, so let me know when you have to go." Her freckles enhance her smile as she sets down another tiny paper cup.

"Great," I say with a short breath out, remembering my first transfer from bed to chair two days earlier. Four nurses, two of them men, surrounded me. After removing the water cast from my right leg, they slowly turned my body, using my battered bottom as an axis. Two held my legs straight and moved them together as a solid mass, and two more supported each side of my body that had been propped fully upright by the bed. Tears formed and I held my breath as the nurses gently brought my feet to a hanging position. I sat and gained my composure. This had been bearable.

"Take all the time you need," the young nurse with the dark

eyes had said. She knew me. She knew me because she had been in the same situation , with others trying to wait out the pain.

I looked at Mom then gave the go-ahead, "Okay, I'm ready."

"On the count of three," the nurse said to me and the others. "One, two, three."

My eyes slammed shut. "Fuck!" I screamed, uncontrolled. "Oh my God! Fuckin' A !"

Tears had streamed down my face as the nurses, two with hands under my knees, one with hands under my left arm and one trying to support my battered right side, lifted my crumpled body to the padded orange chair next to the bed and set me down. I had squeezed my eyelids tight and tried to catch my breath. After my body became accustomed to the new position, I didn't move. For two and a half hours I sat and tried to postpone the inevitable.

I can't image trying to make it all the way to the bathroom. When the nurse leaves the room I close my eyes. Only the hum of the machines remain. I rest my head against the elevated bed, and on the private screen in my mind I watch Mark walk into a large room with soft white walls and gigantic picture windows. He crosses his arms and looks out the window where seagulls swoop, touching the waters that stretch to distant snow capped peaks. His face softens leaving only the hint of a smile and two huge dimples. Then he turns his face to mine.

"This is a perfect place for a reception," he says, arm sweeping toward the glass. "Just look at that view."

"Yes, it's gorgeous and it's a good price too," I add, as I sneak in front of him and pull his arms around me. "They'll let my dad do the catering; otherwise we couldn't afford it."

"It's going to be so fun," he whispers, more to himself than to me, with his chin tucked into my shoulder. It feels so good, I don't want to move. When I finally turn to face him he reaches both hands into the back pockets of my Levi's, and pulls my hips into his. "Can you believe it, babe? We're going to be married."

"Finally. I'm tired of introducing you as my fiancé. I feel like you're already my husband."

"We are husband and wife," he says with mock seriousness, raising his eyebrows. "In our hearts."

I roll my eyes. "Well, we fight like husband and wife sometimes."

"Yeah, but we have fun making up, don't we?" His eyes sparkle as he pulls my hips in tighter. He no longer cares about the reception. "Let's go have some ice cream."

I agree, knowing ice cream is our secret code and knowing he has taken an extra long lunch break.

My mom walks back into the hospital room. She asks how I'm doing and sits down in the chair next to me. I answer her, all the while watching Mark and me move through our lives together. When the nurse walks in, I let the memory fade. The time back in our apartment would be too painful to relive right now. The way Mark held me, the way he kissed the back of my neck as his skin warmed mine. I clench my teeth and tears fill my lower lids as I push it all away. Mom is quiet, her hands resting on mine. I close my eyes and sleep.

Naps become a part of my life. I'm like a baby in more ways than I care to admit. When I wake up this time it's from pressure on my bladder. I'm nervous; with the catheter gone I have to use the toilet. Each move into the chair has been painful, I can't imagine going all the way to the bathroom. My mom, as usual, sits near my bed and is quick to notice my restlessness. She leans closer.

"How are you doing?" she says and gives me her mom smile, the smile that lets me know that I'm loved more than she could ever explain.

"Okay," I answer, out of habit. "But my back is really hurting and I have to go to the bathroom."

"Let me get the nurse," she says. She's out the door before I faintly call her name. She's on a mission. I push the nurse call button. I figure it can't hurt to have us both working on this mission. I am in a hurry.

Mom returns with one nurse. Where's the whole crew?

"This is how it will work," she begins. I try to listen. "I'll transfer you to the wheelchair, and then I'll wheel you to the bathroom door and we'll do another transfer." I nod my head. My situation is getting urgent. "The bathroom transfer will go like this: I'll wrap this strap around your back, under your left arm then up around my shoulders and neck. Then, on three, we'll get you on your feet then you'll need to shuffle about two steps, before you turn your back toward the toilet. I'll use my body to counter your weight and I'll lower you to the toilet seat."

I look at the extra wide martial arts belt, close my mouth tight and breathe in through my nose. "I'm ready," I manage when my lips finally part.

We work together to make the wheelchair transfer. At the bathroom, like two college freshman clinging to one another after a hard night of drinking, we make our way through the door, but I can't reach the toilet.

My frail good leg trembles under the weight of my body.

"I can't do it," I sob.

My good arm is wrapped around her neck and tears soak her shoulder as I cling to her strong body for help. "I can't do it," I repeat each time she tries to lower my bottom to the toilet. Finally, with my body trembling in her arms we stop to rest, exhausted from our awkward dance.

"Oh my God, I forgot to put the riser on the toilet," she says as I'm about to lose control of my bladder. She finds it humorous, and perhaps I will too some day, but I'm not laughing. When the riser is in place, I reach the toilet, dry.

As I open my eyes, angelic green eyes lock with mine. Do I see a halo? I blink. Behind the angel, there is a ghost, a four foot ghost. A cowboy, a ballerina, a witch, Dorothy, and Santa Claus.

"Trick or treat!" escapes from their tiny mouths like a beginning choir. It's been eleven days since life as I knew it ended.

"Hi," I say, using the remote to lift my bed as I reach for the Halloween candies Mom placed nearby. Brightness fills the room. I give each child a Reese's Peanut Butter Cup as they near my bed. I swallow hard when they leave. They will make rounds before they return to their own hospital beds for cancer treatments. I close my eyes but it is hard to sleep.

The next morning I have more visitors. My heart's pounding when they leave and I make sure the door is closed behind them before I allow myself to cry. The two brakemen from the train must have been horrified to find life after such a powerful collision. Had they come to see me now simply to grasp the full extent of what happened? To ease their consciences? Or perhaps to see with their own eyes that I had survived? Whatever the case, their words leave me with painfully vivid pictures.

Propped up in bed I had listened politely. Tired, I'd struggled to focus on the face of the young man closest to the bed. With my vision blurred he could almost have been Mark. I had nodded politely, wondering if this man had a wife he would give his life for. "We blew the whistle," he'd said over and over. I get the picture. I'd closed my eyes. I don't remember hearing a horn, but I don't remember much. I've been hit by a train.

Together the brakemen had continued to describe their dismay. The throwing of the brakes. The screeching of the wheels on the tracks. The look of the man's face before impact. Mark's face. (I'd imagined the fear in Mark's eyes, the realization of the moment.) I'd wanted them to stop talking, but had smiled and nodded as they continued. One man ran the length of three football fields back to the accident site. I'd envisioned him running. Fearful, I'm sure, as I would be, of what he might find.

"I heard a woman screaming and moaning," he'd said. I'd stared through the bouquet of golden dahlias that sat near the foot of my bed on a metal hospital tray. The woman was me. How loud did I scream? Were my clothes still covering my body? I'd continued to stare at the flowers. I'd smiled and nodded. I had new pictures. My mind changed them to movies. I try not to play them, but they run.

The next time I awaken there are a dozen salmon-pink Sonia roses on the bedside table. One more bouquet added to the collection that fills one side of the hospital room. One more glass vase to find a home for, once the flowers have died. I turn to the TV and stare at the screen. A nurse walks in and sets a dinner tray in front of me. I continue to stare at the screen.

"Sonya, you need to eat," my mom coaxes from her chair.

I glance down at the sterile light blue serving tray, set with a cup of milk and several half-filled plastic containers of food. I have no hunger. It has been lost just like my hunger for life. Finally I look up and stare at the machine that helps move blood through my leg. I watch as the machine pumps. Up and down, up and down. I notice the connection between the movement of the machine and a sensation on my leg. Water expands the soft plastic cast that encompasses my right leg. It constricts the muscles in my leg one section at a time from ankle to upper thigh, pushing blood ahead of its path, pushing me to live.

HOME?

Two weeks pass and it is time to leave the hospital. Mom helps me, one limb at a time, to dress in my new sweat suit from Honey and Bampa. The sweats hang from my shrinking body. The occupational therapist has shown me how to use a white plastic form with long straps to pull my socks on, one at a time. To push a sock onto the plastic form with my left hand and drop it down to my foot. To hold the straps and inch my toes into the opening, then pull gently while wriggling my toes around enough to move the sock up my foot. Once the sock is on my foot I am to bend at the waist and with one hand, pull it over my heel and up my ankle. I can't use the damn thing, and it doesn't matter because mom is happy to put on my socks for this special occasion. For friends and family, having me well enough to leave the hospital is a big day. To me it is just another day without Mark.

After gathering the remaining flowers and cards that have been placed in boxes along the floor, my dad looks at Mom and sighs. Now it becomes a waiting game. We wait for the wheel chair taxi. We wait for the nurse who will bring us to it. We wait to sign the final paperwork. The room is silent. I hear my heart pounding. I wait for someone to shake me and tell me it is all a bad dream.

A call comes from the lobby, the cab has arrived. We buzz the nurse just as she is walking in the door with the wheelchair. She explains that we will sign papers on our way out, and then she flashes me a smile: "Let's get you home." I attempt to return her smile; she doesn't realize, however, I'm not going home.

She pushes me down the long hall of the fifth floor. My parents follow. Dad will return for the flowers. With limited vision in my left eye, the hall seems to go on forever in partial darkness. Mom pushes the elevator button and with a ding the metal doors part. My chest tightens. This is real. I hold back tears as we enter the elevator. I study the metal tracks on the floor where the doors slide shut. Everyone else looks to the lighted numbers. There is the usual elevator silence. Time slows as the elevator drops. Ding. The doors open and there is a man in a red polo shirt waiting next to another wheelchair, my wheelchair.

He smiles and introduces himself. I'm tired of smiling, but I smile anyway and give him a raspy "Hello." He and the nurse transfer me to the battered metal rental chair with its brown vinyl seat. The nurse says goodbye and my parents stay to follow me to the taxi. We cross the bare lobby and come to glass double doors, which part. As we roll through them and down the yellow ramp, I squint, my eyes adjusting to the low November sun. As I am pushed along the sidewalk, my parents talk to one another but I don't hear them, instead my body stiffens with each break in the concrete. I want to ask the man to slow down, but he is going slowly. We reach a white van, with bold red letters painted on the side. The van is parked at the top of a steep drive. The drive leads down the hill to a giant metal door centered on a wall of concrete. I don't notice the dappled light that filters through the nearly bare maples and falls upon the side of the van, or the bright letters that spell

72

HEALTHCARE TAXI; my eyes are focused on the driveway. My left knuckles turn white on the arm of my wheelchair. If he loses his grip... My heart pounds. The man who pushes me stops, and then bends down quickly, before reaching up and opening the van door.

"Is the brake set?" I push through my dry throat, before I notice that dad is behind me now holding my wheelchair.

I'm now a spectator in my life and I hate it.

The taxi follows my parents' crimson Ford Taurus away from the hospital and in twenty-five minutes we arrive at my parents' house, the one I left only days ago with Mark by my side. This is my childhood home where I transitioned from Sōn the tomboy to Sonya Gaubinger, the young athletic woman. And though I lived in this house a long time, it seems foreign to me now. My home is with the man I love. My home is with Mark in West Seattle.

Dad parks the Taurus in the small sloping driveway and comes quickly to the side of the van. The driver walks around and opens the door. My wheelchair is strapped to a metal platform that is extended and lowered to the ground. The man releases my wheelchair and releases me to my parents.

"Thanks," I force one last smile.

"Take care," he replies while mom signs more papers. Then he hops in the van and drives away.

My dad pushes me toward the natural stone entry of the house, then turns the wheelchair around backwards and carefully pulls it up each of the three raised landings that lead to the front door. Mom holds the dark wood door open and Dad turns me back around and pushes the wheelchair across the threshold. We bump across the rock entry, pass by the eating nook in the kitchen and stop in the dining room.

"Ready?" Dad asks, looking at my face, then back at the

hospital bed that is sitting smack in the middle of the dining room, the only room large enough to hold it. It is as if the set of a Sci-fi movie has been beamed down to the twelve hundred block of 46th Avenue. This Sci-fi room is now my room.

"No," I say. "Not yet."

I'm tired, but I'm not ready for another transfer. I keep staring at the metal bar that raises high above the bed and see that this nightmare has just begun.

Flowers arrive daily and are added to the ones that line the tall windows overlooking the backyard. Brianna, my cat, who is now at my parents' house as well, thinks this is her jungle and when she is not on my bed she can be found peering through the vases of roses and mixed bouquets, tail twitching.

Over the next week, Mom and I spend hours in the living room, me on Dad's brown corduroy La-Z-boy, and Mom in her soft cream version of the same. She reads me books. Books on grief. Books that, one by one, make me angry. They tell me how to get better. They tell me how loss works. They compare losing a job to losing someone you love. I can't listen.

Nurses and therapists become a part of life at my parents' as well, but much of the time Mom and I simply read, chat and watch TV.

"There's a woman, a counselor named Bonnie, who I thought might be good for you to see," Mom says, looking for a reaction. I stare right through Marlena and Roman on the TV screen and into my past. "She can even come to the house."

"Okay," I answer; nothing can make life better and nothing can make life worse.

"I'll see if she can stop by next week." Mom says.

"Okay." I stare at the TV but see only Mark.

With his lips held tightly together Mark tries not to laugh.

He looks funny holding back his broad smile, but he looks funnier when he no longer can hold his lips together and I see the gap where his front tooth should be.

"I can't believe I lost it." Mark says, as we enjoy a picnic lunch between baseball games. We had driven 400 miles to Canada for a baseball tournament and in the third inning of the first game Mark made a great double play but in the process got hit in the face by a runner who knocked out what was already his temporary front tooth. The game had been stopped briefly to scour the dirt for his tooth, but with no luck. Mark played the rest of the game and would have to play the rest of the tournament, two more days, without a tooth.

"You do look pretty funny," I say before taking a bite of my ham and cheese sandwich.

"Stop it," he laughs, trying to hold his lips together again.

Sitting in Dad's La-Z-Boy I can see Mark so clearly, it's as if he is right in front of me, as if we are together again. I can see him pout while we watch a crew drag the baseball field between the next two games leaving no chance of finding his lost tooth. I can see him searching around second base when he is on the field again, hoping desperately for a miracle, hoping he will find the proverbial needle in a haystack. I can see him reaching down in the dirt, and then holding something so small it is invisible to my eyes, high in the air. He is grinning from ear to ear. Mark found his tooth. Mark was a lucky man or at least I had thought so. I close my eyes and squeeze them tight. Why did this happen to him? Why?

"How are you feeling?" Mom asks.

"Just thinking about Mark," I say. My chest aches and I want to cry. "I think of him all the time. How could this have happened? How can I live without him, Mom?"

Mom crosses the room and pulls up next to me on the arm

of the La-Z-Boy. "I'm here. Your dad and I are here."

"I know, Mom, but I want Mark." Tears flow down my cheeks. "Why did this happen? How could this have happened?"

My mom holds my broken body as it shakes.

Tears run uncontrolled.

Mom dries my tears. I face the TV one more time. The soap opera Another World is playing. I am in another world, one I don't want to live in. I close my eyes and absorb the magnitude of my reality. My body throbs. Mom kisses my forehead and wraps her arms around me. Because of her, and only because of her, I will make it one more day.

WEDDING DAY

Leslie pulls the delicate veil in front of my face. My shoulders still hold a hint of summer and are perfectly accented by the white satin of my wedding dress which drapes in a soft V across my chest.

"You look great," she says.

"Your make-up is perfect," adds Tami-Su.

I think she's right, but I'm not so sure about the hair. I complain about it.

"Shit," Kirsten says. "It took you about two seconds to throw it up with five bobby pins, and it looks awesome." She rolls her eyes and lowers her voice. "Fabulous."

We all laugh; they sure know how to make me feel comfortable.

"You look great," Kris says, resting her hand on my arm.

Lillie, body sunken low into an easy chair, black bridesmaid dress hiked up her thighs, knees touching and the toes of her black pumps pointing at one another, is beaming.

I can see them all, all my bridesmaids. They look great. Look real. I imagine them preceding me down the aisle and then standing by my side, as I promise my love and my life to Mark. I open my eyes and look around the room that is lit by the morning sun. Brianna's on my lap, curled in a tight ball, purring. My leg is hurting from the weight of her body but I can't bear to move her.

Today is my wedding day. Today most of my bridesmaids will come and support me just as they would have done as I prepared to walk down the aisle to marry Mark. Today will be a long day.

Four of my best friends gather around the metal frame of my bed, as I demonstrate the exercises I perform six times a day to strengthen my lungs. I blow into a machine and watch a small white ball rise inside a cylinder, from number one up to number three. Then I use another machine and inhale medicine for my lungs.

"When I first came home from the hospital, I could only get the ball to the number two." I brag, as if I'm talking about last night's basketball game.

"What number do you need to reach?" Kris, my high school basketball buddy, asks.

Kris and I were known as University High School's Gaubinger-Kallestad one-two punch in the local papers; working together we frustrated opposing teams and ended the season tied as the second-leading scorers in the Greater Spokane League.

"I think to the twelve," I answer, knowing for sure it's twelve, but twelve looks too far to reach, to be a number set in stone.

"You'll be there in no time," Leslie says.

"Yeah, it'll be easy," I promise, trying to reassure them and myself, that I will be fine.

Everyone does their best to be cheerful under the circumstances. Two of them have met Mark and all knew how much I loved him. They flew from all over the United States to be with me on what was supposed to be the best day of my life.

Drawing energy from their presence and my Percocet, I share stories. A scar here, a bruise there. Tales from the hospital. I play the perfect hostess from my perch in the center of the bed.

"Why don't you have casts?" asks Tami-Su.

Tami-Su and I were roommates when Mark and I started dating, but I first met the tall blonde with the hour-glass figure in junior high where we played softball together. We made a perfect pair, she pitching and I catching.

"Well," I explain, "there are rods and pins in both my right arm and leg, so they don't need casts." I pull my night shirt up my leg, exposing a bloody strip of tape that runs twelve inches from hip to mid thigh. "It's weird. I guess they put the metal rod right through the center of the bone, and hold it in place with the screws." I look down at my leg again and continue, "I didn't realize that when your bones are in your body, the marrow is liquid, not like a bone on a steak."

Everyone looks on and nods. As a profusionist who regulates blood during heart surgery, Kris already knew this, but everyone else seems to drift back to high school biology for a moment, just as I had, before it sinks in.

If Lillie were here, she would have puckered her lips and brought her forefinger up to them to think about it. She would have stayed that way for a long time, gently caressing her lips, her copper brown hair falling across her shoulders, looking as if she were holding back a question that was bursting to escape. Lilly and I met waiting tables and lived together for three years. She now lives in Chicago and plans to visit me next month.

The day is somehow refreshing. The conversation, superficial in many ways, keeps my attention away from Mark. I absorb their strength, and much to my surprise, I gracefully

79

waltz through my wedding day. The next day, however, the day Mark and I would have traveled to Greece to bask in a romantic paradise of sand and sun on our honeymoon, I sit in silence, buried in grief.

Grief overwhelms my days, and my nights are a barrage of nightmares. I struggle with constant physical pain as each day creeps by. Throbbing and sharp pains penetrate the right side of my body. And I am frustrated with continued double vision and vertigo. But the pain I feel from my injuries doesn't compare to the pain I feel in my heart. It is a physical pain as well as an emotional pain, a pain that radiates straight from my heart, aching and burning, similar I imagine to the pain of a heart attack. If you've lost someone you love, you know the feeling. It is an ache deep within your soul.

My misery is compounded by visions of what could have been. What should have been. I talk with my mom, and others, yet few words enter my mind. Information passes through me like a ghost drifting through a brick wall. Most of my time is spent watching memories of Mark and the times we shared together. They run through my mind, like silent movies, for only me to see. A part of me is desperately trying to hold on to him, hold on to the one person in my life who made me feel complete. Mark was my future and now he is a part of my past. I am numb inside. I welcome death, my death. I hope for an embolism, which can kill me, but doctors feel my recovery looks promising. To me survival looks like a life sentence of misery and pain.

When my eyes are open, I see Mark; when I close my eyes, I see Mark. He haunts me, yet I don't want him to stop. I see us camping on San Juan Island. I see Mark peeking out the door of our tent with his black leather Bulls baseball cap, urging me to join him. I see us walking to the Admiral B & O Espresso for a latte, sitting together at the small sidewalk table.

"This is such a cute neighborhood; wouldn't it be great if someone fixed up that old theater?" I say.

"We should buy it," Mark says, eyes loaded with excitement. "And the corner lot next to it with the rent-a-fence all around it."

I see him dancing to avoid the pile of snapping crab in the bottom of a small black boat. Picking them up two at a time. Laughing and dodging the pincers in the hull of the boat, while the crab he is holding works frantically to free himself from Mark's grip.

I see us smiling at one another, crossing the parking lot hand in hand, on our way to the movie Shattered, the night before the accident. The night before, our lives were shattered.

The honeymoon is long over. It is November 17 and I sit propped in my wheelchair and stare at the TV. The screen is a blur. My mind is a blank. The aching in my soul is unimaginable; the reality of Mark's death and my life without him is sinking in. The hopelessness I feel is overwhelming and I try desperately to hold back my pent-up emotions, when my body begins to shake. The shaking is uncontrollable and I bend at the waist and cover my face with my one good hand. Tears rush down my face. I'm smothered by grief, and gasp with each sob. My mom appears at my side and gingerly places her hand on my shoulder. I keep sobbing. And when I finally look up and see the fear in her eyes as she tries to reassure me, I feel sick inside.

"It's all right," she says in a comforting tone. "It's going to be okay."

I feel the veins in my face begin to pound. With rage directed at life but thrown at my mom, I scream, "It's never going to be okay!" I stare into her caring eyes as hatred boils in mine. "IT'S NEVER GOING TO BE FUCKING OKAY!"

81

Mom keeps her hand on my shoulder for a moment then walks away. I listen to her quick steps down the hall grow faint. She's probably crying too, but I don't care.

A MOTHER'S LOVE

One more sip of water and I swear I'll puke. I'm about to burst and I'm buzzing on a Percocet high that keeps me floating in this unwanted nightmare. More water means another trip to the bathroom, which means another transfer and more pain.

Slumping forward in my wheelchair, my mom rolls me to the table of the dark walnut corner nook (a reminder of my Austrian heritage.) I drop my head and close my eyes. My food and a large glass of water sit untouched. The air behind me thickens and then dissipates slowly as Mom lets out a muffled sigh and walks heavy-footed down the hall to the bathroom. She is unnerved, but I've had four large glasses already, this one can wait.

I've been eating, sleeping, and sitting in my parent's house for thirteen days and I want out. I'm with people I love, but I don't care. I hate my mom for taking a leave of absence from work and being with me all day, for trying to help me get better when I don't want to.

I hate the way the gold wire rims of her glasses accent her caring eyes.

I hate the way she cooks my favorite foods and tries to mask her disappointment when I don't show any enthusiasm.

I hate the way she manages to think of my every need before I do, as a good mother should. And she is a good mother, a great mother, and right now, I hate her for that.

Mom walks back into the kitchen and slips into the corner nook where our family ate all our meals together when I was growing up. Hearty meals prepared from meat my dad brought home from his shop. How'd things go at the shop? Do you have Junior Symphony tonight, Putz? How was basketball practice? I can hear the conversations in my mind. I remember how they lingered in the kitchen as we cleared the blue and white plates with the Bavarian countryside: Putz scraping the last bit of sauerkraut off each dish with the orange scruffy before handing it to me to find a place for it in the dishwasher.

This old kitchen, designed by my mom in the seventies with dark oak cabinets and brown appliances, holds great childhood memories, but now I'm an adult. I'm supposed to be married and starting a family of my own with Mark. I look at the schnitzel, my all-time favorite meal, cold on my plate and my stomach turns.

"Are you feeling okay?" Mom probes, "Maybe you need to take a painkiller."

I push my food awkwardly around my plate with my fork.

"No, I'm fine," I insist, staring at the full plate before I press down on the side of my fork and cut off a small piece of breaded pork. As I chew, a familiar pain creeps into my joints. I put down my fork and take a small sip of water. And as the pain slowly spreads throughout my body, I use my mind to hold it at bay. The pain-killers are addictive, and though I don't want to follow that path, it's not my true reason for abstaining. I want to feel the pain. I want the physical pain to overpower the pain I feel in my heart.

"Mom, I'm done," I say, pushing my plate far enough away

so that I can rest my head on the table. Mom gently caresses the hair from my ponytail that has fallen along side my neck. I'm thinking of Mark. I see him turn and blow me a kiss, touching his leather batting glove to his lips and giving a toss of his hand in my direction on his way to the plate. Not in an arrogant way, just a fun kiss, an I want everyone to know I love you kiss. His tight gray baseball pants hug his full thighs and butt while he moves side to side and settles into his stance before eyeing the pitcher, daring him to throw his toughest pitch.

"Sonya?" My mom touches my arm, interrupting my thoughts.

I fake a smile, trying to convince her I'm okay. "Could you bring me in to the living room to watch TV?"

"Sure, you can finish your lunch later."

When Mom rolls me across the rock entry, the weight of my thigh on the seat of the wheelchair becomes unusually heavy. The constant ache I'm used to is no longer dull. And I'm beginning to feel my heartbeat through my arm as each powerful surge of blood pierces it with pain.

We enter the living room that is just large enough to hold the beige striped couch and the two recliners that face the twelve inch TV with rabbit ears. The fireplace, made of rough natural stone, makes up one wall and loosely separates the living room from the kitchen and dining room. As a kid I used to chase our boxers Prince, Duchess, and Madie around the perfect track with the fireplace at its center; living room, dining room, kitchen, entry, living room, dining room, kitchen, entry. Now I am wheeled slowly around the circular domain.

Leaning back in Dad's La-Z-Boy I stare in disgust at what used to be my favorite soap opera, Days of Our Lives. I used to be able to play along with the characters who died and miraculously came back to life. Now I find it appalling and over time my eyes look focused, but I see nothing at all. I sit staring straight ahead still hoping this is all a nightmare.

I know an hour has passed when I hear, "like sands through the hour glass so are the days of our lives." My life has more than slipped away, and sitting across from my mom, I wonder if I will ever want it back. Trying to relax in her leather recliner and unsure of what to say or do to help make things better for me, Mom looks up as if she is going to ask me a question, but doesn't. She knows that if she were to ask what she could do to help, "Nothing" would be my reply, so instead she tries a different route.

"Let's read for a while," she says, throwing the idea into the air.

"All right," I agree, taking the bait.

Mom reaches to the stack of grief books next to her on the hearth and picks up Living When a Loved One Has Died by Earl A. Grollman. For the first time in a long while I listen.

Your loved one has died.
You are unprepared.
The death has struck like a tidal wave.
You are cut loose from your mooring.
You are all but drowning in the sea of your private sorrow.
The person who has been part of your life is gone forever.
It is final, irrevocable.
Part of you has died.

Grollman is right. I am dead. Without Mark I am dead. Memories are not enough. How does Grollman know? How does he know how I feel inside? I ask Mom to read the passage one more time. I think of Mark's mom and dad…sisters… friends…others reading the book. I am not alone. I know now that I am not alone in my sorrow. I don't feel it, but deep inside, I know it, and it brings me comfort. I close my eyes and see Mark smiling back at me. Tears begin to fall while Mom reads on.

I'm good for about twenty minutes of reading and then it's time for a rest before the first of the healthcare entourage arrive. I decide to forgo my painkiller and after a short nap I awaken in time for the arrival of Shannon, my in-home nurse. Though I don't act like I look forward to her visits, I do. They bring stability to my days. As usual, she asks how I'm doing, and of course I lie. I want to tell her I wish I had died, and I can't live without Mark, but "okay" is what I say. She knows I'm suffering. Why wouldn't I be? So she does her job quickly and kindly and somehow makes me feel better. She checks my vitals, my breathing and my bandages.

Today she's going to remove the tape from the incision on my right shoulder that runs from the top of my shoulder down to my bicep. The tape is nearly four inches in length and underneath its clear surface there is dried blood that reaches across my skin like red wine splattered on pale carpet. I'm not sure I want to see what lies below the bandage but I watch as she peels it back bit by bit. Miraculously, the blood that so boldly lay beneath the surface rises with the bandage and leaves behind an incredibly simple scar. A four-inch thin line, where the rod was inserted and an accompanying half-inch incision for the screw that holds the rod in place. Nothing like I had envisioned. I gain hope that later when they remove the tape on the two huge incisions down my leg, that are held together with twelve large staples, the scars will look better than I expect.

Shannon explains that soon I'll be able to stand and put some weight on my leg. It doesn't seem like much, but she assures me that I'm making good progress. I feel as if I'm sinking slowly into quicksand. I don't want to get better; at least I don't think I do. I wave goodbye to Shannon then ask my mom if she can wheel me back into the living room to watch more TV.

This time the transfer to the La-Z-Boy is tough and I'm so uncomfortable I can't watch TV. I can't even focus on the memories of Mark in my head; all I can think about is the pain.

"Mom, I changed my mind, I need to lie down."

By the time I'm back in my hospital bed in the dining room, I ache all over. Mom kisses me gently and gives me space. I close my eyes and lay very still. Beads of sweat form above my lip and on my forehead. The pressure behind my eyelids builds slowly until it becomes unbearable. My body is on fire. Tears fill my eyes.

"What's wrong?" Mom asks appearing at my bedside.

"Nothing," I sob.

"I'm calling the doctor," she says, resting the back of her hand on my forehead. "You've had your flu shot. Something's not right."

I hear my mom's muffled voice in the kitchen. She hangs up the phone and then she scurries about before returning to my bed carrying a big glass of water. What I can't see in her other hand are two Percocet. I've discovered the hard way that I need to keep up with the pain. To control it or it will take over. I thought that it was what I wanted, but I was wrong, it was more than I can handle.

By the time my dad comes home from the shop and Mom has made dinner, the painkillers have done their job and I'm ready to rest. After dinner my parents put me to bed and go into their room so I have some privacy. Tonight I hope to dream of Mark. I haven't yet, so I don't expect to. I just hope.

Instead, I cry myself to sleep only to be awakened by pressure on my bladder. Dad is a light sleeper so in my raspy voice, which is scarcely audible due to my punctured lung, I call to him. I wait, but he doesn't appear.

"Daaaddd," I try again, this time with more urgency.

Three more times and I can't hold back tears. Mom won't

hear me she's such a heavy sleeper. The thought of wetting myself and lying in it the rest of the night disgusts me. But I give up my meek efforts to call and simply cry.

"Sonya?" Mom appears out of the darkness.

"Mom, I've gotta go to the bathroom."

"Okay, let's get you out of that bed," she says, gently pulling back the covers, she moves my wheelchair to the side of the bed for my transfer and puts the right arm of the chair parallel to the bed frame on my left. It is butted tight against the frame of the bed, brake set. I look up at the metal triangle that hangs above my head. The simple triangle handle is an intricate part of my progression from lying to sitting. But first my mom has to move around to the right side of the bed and gingerly remove the wrap that keeps blood flowing through my battered right leg twelve hours a day. Then coming back around to my left she raises the hospital bed to a sixty-degree angle. Using the small metal handle, I make the most of my minimal arm strength and with some help from my mom; I lift and reposition myself near the edge of the bed for the transfer, all the while working desperately against the urge to pee.

"Mom, I don't know if I can make it," I say squeezing back tears.

"Sure you can," she says reaching around my back and under my arms as I skooch a little further to the left. My right arm is held tight into my body with a sling and my mom gently holds my legs as I take a deep breath before pivoting on my bruised bottom. I turn until my legs come to the side of the bed where my mom lowers them slowly. Both legs are now withered and dangle from the side of the bed like a puppets wooden legs, I don't recognize them as mine.

"Mom," I cry.

"Just hang on," she says, "we're almost there."

I'm grateful I've taken my painkillers as we hurry down

the hall to my parent's bathroom, the only bathroom the wheelchair can fit into and is set with a riser. We make it just in time for a dry transfer to the toilet.

I'm sitting in the La-Z-Boy watching TV as my body withers away. Dad has gone to work at the shop after our quick breakfast together and now I simply wait. Wait for the next bout of tears when life again becomes unbearable. The local news breaks with a headline story from Mark's home town of Everett. A boy on his bike is killed, hit by a train. I can't believe it. Just last week, there was another fatal car/train accident, when a driver had attempted to outrun the train to the crossing.

"Mom," I raise my voice, "did you hear that?"

Mom walks into the living room carrying a stack of books.

"What?" she looks with concern, and then follow my eyes to the TV screen.

"A kid was killed in Everett. Hit by a train. I can't believe how often it happens."

"That's awful," my mom says watching the recap of the top news story. "Let's turn this thing off."

She grabs the remote on the way to her chair and gives it a push. She is quiet. Finally she pulls out a book with blue and white floral fabric for the cover. I realize it's a journal. When she brings it to me, I thank her for it and set it aside.

"I hope you'll try writing in it," she is cautious with her request. "Remember, Bonnie thought it might be a good idea."

Up to this point the counselor's advice has gone unheeded.

A week creeps by. I'm now sleeping in the bed I used in high school and have gotten rid of the contraption in the dining room. It's hard to get out of the old low-slung single bed, but having a firm mattress, one on slats, not a springy hospital mattress, is worth it. It's just what my aching back needs.

As Dad wheels me into my room to go to bed, I notice the floral journal on the edge of the desk and ask dad to wheel me to it and then ask for a pen. Dad returns with an old blue Bic, sets it in front of me and gives me a goodnight kiss. The scent of pine follows him out the door. When the door is closed, I reach for the pen with my left hand, and carefully switch it to my right. Gripping the pen awkwardly with my weakened hand, I'm barely able to hold the journal in place while I drag the pen across the page with my broken limb. But once I begin to write, all the pain I've held inside floods the pages. I write the obvious. I write the unthinkable. And as tears stream down my face, I write to save my life.

I sleep well. I haven't slept better since being hit by the train, but even with good sleep, I wake to a bad day. The pain in my heart is nonstop and so is my crying. I decide to make a list of all the great times Mark and I shared. I hope it will help me feel better. But for some reason I'm afraid to write. Afraid that if I write down everything about Mark, it's proof that he is gone forever. That I must write it all down to hold on to those parts of him I don't ever want to forget. The drive over the North Cascade Highway, where we stopped at nearly every mile marker to take pictures and enjoy the view. The hike to the top of San Juan Island where we admired the fading suns' painted sky. I want to hold these memories, and all the rest, tight, just as I wish I could hold Mark.

Finally, I take a deep breath and lower my pen to the next page of my journal and begin to write, listing everything that comes to my head. The list grows quickly, but seems stale and empty. Just words. Nothing that emulates the vibrancy that is so much a part of each story, but I keep writing anyway, until each story plays in my mind, and I realize that the list is my only hope for saving all those beautiful moments. To be able to play them back in my mind when many years have passed. The list grows and grows and I hardly notice the knock at the door. Moments later Denise, my physical therapist, walks up behind me.

"How's your body feeling today?" she asks bending down so I can see her on my left.

"Well," I begin, as I close my journal quickly and tuck it beside me on my wheelchair. "I've been putting weight on my leg and it feels okay."

"That's good," she says.

"I should say, it doesn't hurt any more than usual."

"That's to be expected." She waits and listens.

"I still can't really move my arm much; it just throbs and aches all the time. But I just moved into my old bed and I think it's going to be better for my back. I couldn't stand the hospital bed; it was killing me."

"I'm not surprised," she smiles and stands up to push my wheel chair away from the window, "I'll help you with your stretches and exercises and then I'll give you a massage. Sound good?"

"The massage does, I could skip the rest." I try, knowing it will never happen.

After physical therapy I'm ready for my massage. Sitting in my chair, Denise glides her skilled hands along my spine and explores the tension that spreads across my back. As she works I close my eyes and think of Mark. It stirs my emotions until I can no longer hold back tears. Denise is used to my tears. She works in silence. How is it that I'm able to survive? Each day drags on with such pain and sorrow, while the rest of the world goes on living as if everything is okay. How can life ever be okay again? I inhale and slump further into the chair. Denise's strong hands move over my tender flesh, helping release the tension of body and mind. Ever so slowly, the pain inside subsides and as I shed my last tear, I know I will survive one more day.

I look up into Denise's face. It's touched with freckles. She looks back warmly, not with the pity-laced smile that I've learned to expect. She touches my hand, holding my attention with eyes that know of a million sad stories. Then she lowers herself to my eye level, and with both of her hands she holds my good hand tight.

"How's that?" she smiles.

"Good," I return her smile, "thank you."

"I'll be back in two days. Make sure you get up on your leg at least three times a day, just stand and put pressure. Not side to side yet. Keep having your mom lift your arm away from your body, even if it's just an inch, and one more week with the lung machine, and then I think you should be finished with that." She squeezes my hand. "Take care; see you on Thursday."

She walks to the front door, says good-bye to my mom and lets herself out.

Walking up to my wheelchair, Mom bends down and gives me a kiss. Then pushing me into the living room she helps me into Dad's chair and cranks up the footrest so I can lay back to watch the end of yet another soap opera. I close my eyes for a short while, then try to focus on the colored pixels that dance across the screen. Instead I see Mark alive and in full color. I'm not sure how long I can continue down this imaginary road, but I'm going to keep driving it as long as the movies will run. I live for them now; memories are all I have.

"Mom?" I question, without looking up.

"Yes Sonya," Mom answers, glancing from her chair next to the fireplace.

"Could you shave my legs?" I ask. There is a constant itching from my thighs that have rarely gone a day without the touch of a razor. "I can't stand it anymore."

Mom walks over to the La-Z-Boy, leans forward and sets her hand on my good leg, "Sure I can."

After I'm in the wheelchair, Mom pushes me down the hall to the bathroom. It's tight in my parent's bathroom with two people and a wheelchair, but it's the easiest place to shower since it doesn't have a tub to contend with. Mom grabs the medical shower stool, purchased with all the other devices that help me to get through life, and though it isn't easy to complete the tight transfer into the three foot-by-three foot stall, we manage. Once on the stool I look at my body. It is so thin I hardly recognize it as my own. My rail-like thighs and boney knees with protruding goose bumps truly fit the name I carried in middle school, Chicken Legs. I never thought I had chicken legs then, but now I have chicken legs. I am Chicken Legs.

Once my legs are shaved, Mom moistens a washcloth and carefully washes my face. My black eye is gone and so is the big scab above my lip. But for the empty glaze to my eyes, one might say my face is perfect. I wish it were scarred to show the way I feel inside.

I slump forward with hands held together in my lap while Mom runs the soapy washcloth across my back. I stay this way as she takes the hand-held shower and rinses away the soap. I can barely breathe and sit motionless, hoping the water will wash away my sorrow and everything that has happened.

"Are you alright?" Mom asks trying to hold the water steady while standing cramped along side me in the tight space.

"Yeah," I answer out of habit, before I slowly sit up. Mom dabs the wash cloth around the incisions on my broken arm. Steam fills the shower. I close my eyes. This can't be happening

94

to me. Mom carefully washes my chest and legs before turning off the water. She hangs up the shower nozzle then leans down and presses her lips to my forehead.

"Sonya, I love you so much," she whispers.

I look up at her with tears in my eyes.

Mom senses my every need. She knows she can't fill the important ones, because they all have to do with Mark. But she tries and today, I love her for that.

FINDING MY GAME FACE

I'm in Montana. The soft blue sky opens to the heavens and extends to all ends of the earth and is dusted with ever-changing puffs of white. Sitting on an old wooden bench watching the white clouds drift effortlessly across the sky, I breathe in slowly and close my eyes. With eyes shut, I see the brilliant glow of blue as my body sinks into the bench. I sit quietly for a long time before someone slips onto the bench next to me. I'm not surprised; with my eyes still closed, I simply take another breath and sink further into the bench. With that breath, I breathe in Mark. Mark has been dead for more than a month but his masculine scent is unforgettable and leaves me frozen. Afraid, I slowly open my eyes and my breath catches in my throat at the sight of his beautiful face. The sparkle in his eyes and the curl of his lips call to me, asking me to believe. Without a word I tentatively reach down to touch the strong thigh that belongs to the man I have been missing so desperately. There is a sensation of warmth when my fingers touch his skin. Mark is alive!

The shock I feel inside is returned in his wide eyes. He grabs me hard and pulls me tight engulfing me in his strong arms. The moment is cut short when he releases his hold and moves his hands gently to my face. With one of them he traces every feature, following the movement with his eyes. Longingly he runs his finger along the curve of my temple to my forehead above my eyebrow and down the bridge of my nose. Lingering on my lips, he finally reaches my chin and looks up. He leans into my aching body, and gives me a kiss. It's a long kiss, but not nearly long enough. And when he lets me go ever so gently, I stare in disbelief. Suddenly he throws his arms high above his head and screams at the top of his lungs, "I'm alive!"

Mark jumps up and begins to run and I feel the life drain from my body as he disappears into the distance.

The pain in my right arm awakens me. I pry my eyes open and the glowing red numbers on the clock, tell me it's 4:58 a.m., the usual time when my pain medication can no longer hold off the pain and my body fights to find comfort. Although I've graduated to sleeping on my left side, which is an improvement over sleeping on my back, it's only because I'm a side sleeper. My right leg is propped up with two pillows to keep the thighbone parallel to the mattress and my right arm is propped with more pillows from nearly every angle to keep it virtually immobile. Both are now throbbing with pain and I need painkillers soon. But I don't move. I want relief from the pain but I also want to dream of Mark again. I close my eyes and try, but he is gone now, even in my dreams.

Just as the morning light strikes the bedroom window my tears are finally gone. Squeezing my eyelids tight I push the pillows from under my arm onto the floor. Then using every bit of strength in my left arm, I lift myself to a seated position. The walls spin. Tired of the room moving every time I sit up or lay down, I try to ignore it. But I can't ignore it anymore than I can ignore the pain I feel in my heart. I can only go on, knowing it's there, and knowing that as much as I'd like it to, the pain will not kill me.

I lift my body from the bed and reach for the quad cane

that's replaced my wheelchair. It's a slow journey to the bathroom and when I'm done I find myself turning right, instead of left, when I exit through the door. The house is silent except for a faint snore. My arm throbs, but my heart is throbbing more. I must be having a heart attack, please let it kill me. I slide my right foot silently across the carpet and move to the end of my parents' bed. The shades are drawn and I can hear my own belabored breathing.

I step closer. "Mom?" I whisper. "Dad?" By the time the words leave my mouth both are staring wide-eyed in my direction.

"Are you okay?" Mom asks.

"Yes, my arm hurts, but," I look down for a moment then continue, "can I get in?"

"Sure," she folds back the feather duvet and crawls from the bed, her long peach nightgown flowing to the ground. "Dad can help while I get pain-killers."

Dad rests my cane against the wall and then helps me to the side of the tall bed. We wait for mom and the painkillers, and then we all work together to get my body to the center of the bed. My parents slip in beside me in their respective places, the warmth of their bodies soothing my mind. Enough to perhaps sleep again. The duvet is tucked up under my chin and very few words are spoken. I close my eyes and tears reach their corners. As with nearly every moment of my life, my thoughts are on Mark, but lying here between my parents somewhere deep in my heart I'm grateful to be with them.

❋

Other than a nice dinner of turkey and gravy, Thanksgiving goes unnoticed. One and a half months have gone by since the accident. My mom, my constant companion, returns to work. My other companion, the TV, is on, but still barely holds my attention. I feel lonely and empty inside, but at the same time

I'm relieved to be alone. Day by day my mom's constant hovering has stripped away some unknown part of me that makes me feel like an adult. I love her, but I've begun to suffocate under her care.

It's nice to cry to an open room. To have the empty space filled with my sorrow. To sit and think of Mark and know my daydreams will not be interrupted. I want to live in the past; a future without Mark is unthinkable. Sitting on the couch, my quad cane propped nearby, I look down at my ring finger and reach to the gold band. I spin the crystal clear diamond around and around. Mark chose the perfect engagement ring. A solitaire set on a simple gold band. Moving my fingers to the adjacent band I spin both the wedding band and the engagement ring. We had designed the wedding bands with the diamonds set low for durability, and really to play basketball. Mark never got the chance to see the wedding bands, and more painful to imagine, he and I would never play basketball again. Staring at my finger, cheeks wet with tears, I promise myself I will wear this ring forever and I will never get married.

The phone rings and interrupts my thoughts. I look at my cane and question whether I should make the effort, then scoot to the edge of the sofa. Using the cane I pry my body from the couch and slowly make my way into the kitchen to answer the phone. The phone rings again and again; my parents don't have voice mail or a message machine, so I have plenty of time to reach the phone if the caller doesn't hang up.

"Hello. Gaubinger residence," I answer, trying to sound chipper. (It was ingrained in my upbringing.)

"Hi Sonya, how are you doing?" rings through the line.

"Oh, pretty good," I say. My patent response.

This call is the first of many such calls throughout the overcast and dreary winter day, as friends and family check in on me. Most don't know it is my first day home alone. I know for certain that Mark is taking care of me, that he is by my side. I feel him as I hobble to the kitchen to make my own ham-and-cheese sandwich. I feel him as I do my leg lifts and arm exercises. I feel him with each laboring trip to the phone. But most of all I feel his presence when I cry. Perhaps trying to assure me that one day every thing will be all right.

With all the support throughout the day, and partially from it, by day's end I'm exhausted. Dad comes home from the shop early and after Mom arrives we sit around the table and exchange stories about our day over dinner. But it's not long before I say goodnight. I'm tired and after jotting a quick note in my journal, I know I will sleep.

I pry my eyes open and look at the clock. Right on time, 5:07a.m. Lying still I listen to my body, listen to the pain. I can't remember what it's like to feel normal. Even worse I can barely remember what it's like to feel Mark. I can remember him running his fingers through my hair as I kiss and caress his strong chest. But I can't feel it and, God, I want to feel it, feel him. Feel his hands run down my back and pull my hips close to him. I want to make love to him, feel him inside me, a part of me.

Sometimes I convince myself that I'm pregnant, knowing that it would be the only way I could keep a part of him with me forever. Mark and I had made love on our last day together. I still haven't had my period. I'm certain it's impossible to be pregnant after what my body has been through, yet it seems impossible to be hit by a train, so I hope.

Now that I can get out of bed myself, each morning begins with a slow struggle as I wade through stacks of pillows in search of freedom and the side of the bed. And with each morning, life brings a new twist on the subject of pain. My arm and leg are always at varying degrees of extreme pain.

Then there are the "other pains." Yesterday my right foot was throbbing and my neck was bound. This morning my lower back is killing me and I'm suffering from vertigo, so I use my left arm to push my body upright then sit and let the dizziness go away. Waiting for my body to right itself, I reach up with my left hand to rub my eyes awake and I'm startled by my rough skin. Like fine sandpaper the skin on my face almost scratches my hand.

"Mom," I call to the far bedroom

I hear an urgent, but muffled, "yes," come from my parent's room.

"Something's wrong with my face," I say, at nearly a whisper as I touch every bit of my face as if I were blind.

"What's wrong?" mom asks, as she rushes into my room donning her long turquoise robe.

"Look at my face," I say, forehead raised.

"It looks fine, Sonya," she answers with a sigh of relief.

"No, come closer and feel it," I try again.

"Hmmm," Mom says, as she softly runs her fingers across my face, "It looks like you've got a rash."

"Great." I roll my eyes, "one more thing."

"I'll call the doctor, after breakfast, it's probably from the pain killers," she says.

"Mom, I'm hardly taking any pain killers anymore, remember."

"I'm sure it'll be fine," Mom says, kissing me on my bumpy forehead. "Do you want to try to go back to sleep or are you ready to get up?"

"I'm ready to get up," I answer, running my fingers across my face one last time.

Shannon and Denise come and go and by dinner I'm snapping at my mom like a turtle. It's not a surprise when the doctor suggests that my sandpaper face is a product of stress. I use my cane to get to the living room and lower myself into my resting place and stare at the TV.

"Would you like to go for a walk?" Dad asks, drying his hands on the dish towel. He's finished with the dishes, now he's ready for a walk.

"No," I answer.

"Well, I need a walk, and so does Madie," he says and I know he fully intends on pushing me along.

He brings out my socks and shoes and sits on the coffee table in front of me to put them on.

"How are things at the shop?" I look to his face. There is a furrow in his brow before he looks up from my shoe.

"Slower than last year, but with Christmas coming it should pick up."

Dad rolls the wheelchair—that's been banished to the back room for use during long excursions—into the entry way. It's been a mild winter, so it's been easy to roam the neighborhood together. No snow on the ground in Spokane in December is unheard of. Though Dad would have pushed me through the snow if he'd had to, I like to think that Mark is taking care of me, making sure I can get out for fresh air. And today, the scent of Ponderosa Pine is crisp in the air and my mind begins to clear.

"Dad?" I ask.

"Yes?" he answers pushing hard to get up Van Marter Street.

"Mom's driving me crazy," I say, looking down at the green plaid blanket that covers my legs.

"She's worried about you," he says.

"I know," I whine, "but I can't stand it, she's not even there all day. I just can't stand it anymore, Dad. I'm twenty five years old and..."

My throat grows tight and tears burst to the surface.

"I just want Mark back! How could this have happened, Dad? Why did this happen to me? I don't know if I can stand it, I just want him back!"

Dad stops the wheel chair briefly, and rests his hands on my shoulders.

"I know Sonya," he whispers. "I know."

Then he pushes on knowing the pain is there and allowing it to be there. It's quiet and we move forward, just as I will have to do with my life.

Brianna lies on my bed, waiting patiently, but instead of crawling into bed, I cross the room, lean my cane against the desk and sit down. I pick up a pen and stare at the cover of my journal. My journal is filled with entries. Most of them speak of misery and a shattered life. But they all help me sleep at night. They all dry my tears before my head hits the pillow, and for that I am thankful. I open to a blank page.

December 13, 1991

Today was terrible, I cried all day. It still seems so unreal. Mark and I were so in love. We had such a bright future together. I can't believe it's all gone. I miss Mark so much, he was my best friend in the world and now, when I need him most, he's not here. We could have made it through anything together but now I'm all by myself. I don't think I can do it.

The tears flow uncontrolled. I don't want to go on with my life, without Mark, but I need to find a way. I lift my good arm and drag it across my face and then lower my head to the desk. My body heaves until over time the tears subside and I lift my head and begin again.

*I'm going to Seattle on the 17th. It will be good to
see Mark's family but it'll be hard. I keep envisioning
myself standing by Mark's gravesite with a bouquet of
Sonia roses, the kind we were supposed to have in our
wedding, and collapsing in tears. Of course I couldn't
collapse because it would hurt too much, so I'm sure
I'll just stand there and cry and make anyone around
me uncomfortable. I don't know if I'll be able to take
it? God I want Mark back. I miss him so much.*

I end my journal with my usual note to Mark:

Dear Mark-

*Thank you for watching out for me. I know you're
with me, I can feel it, but it's still so hard, I don't know
if I can go on.*

Maybe, with time, and your strength, I will make it.

I miss you so much!

Love,
Sonya

My parents take time off work to drive me to physical
therapy. I'm ready for more. I work on healing my body, and
though it's nothing like the rehabilitation from my sports
injuries of the past it gives me a focus. The therapists use the
same machines, the electric muscle stimulators and ultrasound
machines from my past, but the pain is different. The first
time my Mom helped with PT exercises at home, the nurse
had asked her to gently lift my bad arm out from my body. Ten
times, five times a day. When she tried, I had screamed as she
lifted it a half an inch. I was used to lifting thirty pounds in a
single arm bicep curl; I was used to pulling rebounds off the

boards and tossing up twelve footers from the baseline. I was not used to thinking of a half an inch as an accomplishment, especially when it hurt.

That was in the beginning, and now, three times a week, I find myself wading into a pool and allowing the water to cradle my arm as it leaves my side. I find myself chatting with Kevin, my physical therapist, at the pool and with Laurie while I ride the bike and receive my massage. I find myself making it through each day, one day at a time.

Physical therapy was hard today. Limping into the locker room with my head hung low, I find my locker and slowly lower myself to the wooden stool made of pine. I reach up and slide the blue strap of my new swimsuit off my shoulder. Fortunately Mom found a swimsuit with a low back so that the straps slip off easily. I carry my swimsuit into the shower and hang it on the pull. I step into the shower and the water rolls down my back, soaking my long blonde hair. Why is it that life goes on when you don't want it to? How have I made it this far when I wish I had breathed my last breath? The water is hot, but I get goose bumps as a light breeze moves the shower curtain in the tiny stall. Someone must have entered the locker room. It had better not be my mom. I envision her sprinting in to the locker room to see what is taking so long. To see if I've fallen and cracked my head open on the white tile floor. What if I had slipped, hit my head just right and killed myself falling in the shower? I survive being hit by a train, but die taking a shower. The hint of a smile parts my lips. Sonya, it's not funny! Nothing is funny. Mark can't be laughing and having fun anymore, so neither can you.

For that matter, how can anyone smile? It isn't fair. Don't people know how terrible life can be? My face grows hard again. Don't they know? No one knows how alone you can feel, how alone I feel. Not Mom, not anyone. I can't stand it any more; I can't stand being around people. Like that asshole at Albertsons yesterday, who stood in line complaining. I just wanted to scream, "Shut the fuck up! Don't you know life can be a hell of a lot worse than waiting in a slow line?" I wanted to lean forward onto my cane, maybe even hit him with it first, and tell him how terrible life can be. How unbearable it is when you have to live without the person you love. "You think you've got it bad," I'd say, the words dripping with sarcasm, "I got hit by a 2000-ton locomotive. Yeah, a train. And if that's not bad enough," I'd continue, pronouncing each word slowly, my eyes burning his, "it was just days before my wedding and my fiancé was killed." Mark, I can't stand it anymore. I miss you so much! How am I supposed to go through this, through life, without you?

Steam lingers in the open shower. Tasting the familiar salt on my lips, I struggle to gain composure and fight back the inevitable heaves that accompany my tears. Finally I raise my left arm to cover my contorted face and give in to the sorrow. I cry until my tears are gone, and then standing under the hot water I wash before I turn off the shower. I feel as if my grief, at least for the moment, has been washed away. I gather myself to face the day, putting each piece of clothing on step by step in a slow methodical way, but at least I can now dress myself.

I use my left hand to dig in the bottom of my black duffle bag and come up with a brush first, and then a hair dryer. I make my way cautiously to the mirror and find myself staring into the face of a broken woman. The reflection I see is of a body void of promise. Once self reliant and strong willed, I was a woman who spoke her mind and carried her own bags. Now I struggle to take even a small step. Squinting my eyes, I search the mirror again for that gutsy player who wasn't intimidated by guarding a six-foot man, who in fact enjoyed the challenge.

I look hard into the mirror to find that lost "game face." That set jaw and narrowed eyes that scream determination. I take a long slow breath in through my nose then open my mouth and let the air escape my body, blinking away new tears that try to find a home.

Drying my hair on high, I brush through it as best as I can with my left hand. Then bending at the waist I move my head as far to the right as possible. I have a "frozen shoulder", and my right arm now hangs awkward and stiff like a broken branch, sticking out from my body at a 45-degree angle. I bend my right elbow and reach my right hand along side of my head, bringing my left hand over to meet it. Clumsily my hands work together to pull my fine hair back and forth through a soft elastic band. Straightening up I look in the mirror and smile. It's not a game-winning shot in the playoffs or a ribbon at a state track meet; it's a simple ponytail that falls lazily off my right shoulder. But it's the first time I have been able put my hair in a ponytail by myself since the accident and it leaves me with a sense of accomplishment that I haven't felt in a long time.

RIDE TO FREEDOM

I'm sitting in a dining room chair at my parent's house doing home exercises for my leg and Mark is dead. It seems surreal. I lift my foot out in front of me and tighten my quadricep. After having shrunk to nothing my muscles are finally gaining strength. I've stopped using the machine for my lungs. They're healed now, and instead I focus on exercises for my leg and arm that I'm supposed to do several times a day, everyday at home, in addition to physical therapy at the hospital.

Finishing the last set of ten, I think back to the book Mom and I read last week. It suggested writing a letter to say good-bye to your deceased loved one, but I can't do it. I know Mark is never coming back, but I'm not ready to say good-bye. The book also suggested writing down goals. I used to set goals all the time for basketball but right now it seems impossible.

I complete my leg work and move on to arm exercises. My mind swirls with fading memories of Mark. I want them to be clear. I want to see his face, his eyes, his lips. I want them and him to be real again. I lift my arm gently; moving it to nearly a 90-degree angle from my body, then back down slowly. I wish Mark were here, he would help me get better. I know he wants me to get better, I feel it in my heart. Maybe I can set some goals. Goals to help heal my body. I decide to write them in my journal. My first goal will be to drink a lot of water and do my exercises every day. But I need a goal I can hold on to, one like winning a tournament or getting 25 points and 10 boards. I decide I will walk without a cane in one month. I can do that, I know I can.

One thing I'm not sure I can do is visit Mark's grave. I'll be visiting his family soon and Mark's grave is nearby. Part of me wants to go, but part of me is afraid. Afraid that seeing his grave will make his death final. There will be no more hoping that he might walk through the door. I'll see that his body has a place in the ground and a stone honoring his time here on earth. Sonya, you have to do it, you have to visit Mark's grave.

The five-hour trip with Dad, from Spokane to Everett seems longer than usual. The painkillers hold back the pain, but barely. When we finally arrive, I step out of my parents' car, lean on my cane and close the door. Though this is Mark's parents' house, Mark is here. He is in the yard, in every hallway, in every room. While driving here I couldn't remember what the house looked like; I had always been looking at Mark. And now that I'm here, it all comes back to me. I'm still standing, staring, when Larry throws wide the front door. He steps side to side down the narrow stairs that lead to the house and is next to me before I can take a step, helping me to the door. Dad says hello and follows with my duffle.

We gather in the living room where Larry and Joan are meeting my dad for the second time. The first was when they came to visit me in Spokane after Mark's funeral. What a difficult visit that must have been for them. I had felt ashamed to be alive and they had treated me like a daughter. And now welcoming me into their home, they share stories about Mark that I've never heard and I love it. Mark and I had only spent

110

eight months together, so there was a lot about him I didn't know. I hardly knew Larry and Joan. I had assumed I would have the rest of my life with Mark and with them. I had assumed that after becoming their daughter-in-law I would have the opportunity to become closer to them. I glance at Dad. My family and friends didn't know Mark. Only a few had briefly met him. It's good to be here. I realize that it's been hard to be alone in my grief.

Dad doesn't stay long. He has to get back to Spokane, and the shop. I will spend a few days with Mark's family, and then Mom will come to Seattle and drive me back to Spokane. After I wave goodbye to Dad, Larry asks if I'd like to go to Mark's grave. My palms begin to sweat. I say yes. The cemetery is not like I'd imagined. The tombstones are flat to the ground, trees are sparse and there are large rhododendrons throughout the manicured grass. We pull up to the curb. I don't want to get out. I hold a dozen peach roses tight on my lap with my left arm and take a deep breath. Larry comes around to help me out of the car then leads me carefully by the stone slabs that show this world that a life has come and gone, and finally to the stone that does the same for Mark. The inscription reads:

We Love You OV
Mark Alan Overholt
Dec 24,1965 - Oct 20, 1991
We'll miss your smile

Tears stream down my face. I can't move. I just stare, the roses hanging by my side.

"He was a great guy," Larry says, voice cracking, looking at the place where his son's body lay deep in the ground.

"I miss him so much, Larry," comes bursting out, my body shaking.

Reaching his arm around me Larry whispers the same, and together we cry until there are no more tears.

It's been good to be with Mark's family, to celebrate Debbie's 21st birthday in the limo Mark had been saving for, to play bingo with Grandma and Grandpa Lowry, and to visit with Mark's friends, the friends whom I'd thought would one day be mine. But as good as it's been to be with the Overholts, the flood of memories and tears leave me drained and I look forward to being back in Spokane, except for the fact that it's almost Christmas.

Christmas, to me, is the twenty-fourth of December, it's the day I grew up celebrating. It's also Mark's birthday. Mark would have been twenty-six. We would have been married, expecting a baby if we were lucky. But we weren't lucky. And now I will be spending Christmas, and Mark's birthday, without him.

Back in Spokane we have a moment of silence for Mark before Christmas dinner. I think about what we might have done. Where would we have spent Christmas? I imagine what it would have been like to have spent Christmas, and Mark's birthday, at my parent's home with Mark by my side. It would have been nice to have my dad welcome him into our family and our Christmas traditions with a toast. It should have been that way. A part of me still can't believe I'm sitting here without him. I take a bite of the perfectly roasted turkey, with mashed potatoes and gravy, one of my favorites, and I chew each gravy laden piece of turkey as if it weren't there. When I speak, my chest aches. I move through the evening, giving and receiving presents with an empty heart. Christmas, and Mark's birthday, come and go like every other day, in waves of numbness and tears.

I try to slam the door with my good arm. I can't stand it here, with my parents, especially with my mom. I can hear Dad talking in a hushed voice to her. She's crying. I don't care. I want to live my own life, make my own decisions. I want to go play basketball, walk Green Lake, hold Mark in my arms. I want it all back. I move slowly across the floor to my bed and crawl in. I did such a superb job slamming the door that Brianna is able to push the door with her nose and come join me. At least I'm not crying. Because it seems like I'm always crying and because sometimes when I cry Brianna bites me. I like to think she does it because she doesn't like to see me upset. Maybe I just ruin her naps. Whatever the case, I don't have to worry about it right now, I'm just mad. With my door now open, I can hear Mom. She doesn't know what to do for me. She wants to make it all better. I don't care, I just want out of this house. I want to be on my own. I don't hear Dad's soft voice reassuring her; "This is a good thing, Carole. Her fighting is a good thing."

I watch the ball drop in Times Square (volume turned down). Dick Clark's unheard voice is undoubtedly making the countdown while I sit in the living room with Mom and Dad. There are fireworks exploding outside in celebration of the New Year. I see Mark and me on the rooftop of my apartment, watching Fourth of July fireworks, so long ago. Tears won't stop. I wait until the ball drops, then I kiss Mom and Dad, pick up my cane and make my way to my room. I sit on the edge of the bed and begin the slow processes of getting my clothes off and my pajamas on. When I'm done, I rest my cane near the bed and limp across to the desk. Sitting in the chair, I begin to write.

January 1st, 1992

The year 1991 was the best and the worst year of my life. I met the man of my dreams and then I lost him

113

and lost everything. Each day just gets harder and harder. I know Mark would want me to go on, but it doesn't seem like I can. I want Mark back, I want our life back!

I make a tight fist then drop my head to the desk and soak the pages of my journal. Why did this have to happen? Why do I have to go on?

Dear Mark,
Life is so meaningless without you. I would do anything to be with you again. Please give me strength; it is so lonely without you here.

I love you!
Sonya

*

I open the car door slowly as if to curb the flow of adrenaline that's rushing through my body. Balancing deftly on my left foot and using my left hand I slide my cane across the driver's seat of the Taurus and brace it against the cushion of the passenger's seat. My cane unknowingly becomes an accomplice to my escape. The open driver's seat tugs on my mind, drawing from my memory of the look on Doctor Coulton's face, in the hospital, only months ago.

"I'll just pick up my wheelchair and set it next to me in the passenger seat," I had explained.

Dr. Coulston's face concealed nothing, including the urge to laugh at such an absurd comment. A comment that was based on what my life and body had been, not the broken and battered person who had been hit by a train only days earlier.

"Sonya," he'd said with a straight face, "you won't be driving for a long time."

Why not? A few more days and I'll be fine.

"Even when you're able to get into a car comfortably, you can't risk re-injuring your arm," he'd explained.

I smile. I feel like the rebel that I've never been. I reach down and grab the leather steering wheel with my left hand. No, not going to work. Trying again I grip the roof, where the door would be, and gently lift my right leg into the car between the seat and the steering wheel. Like a 90-year-old stroke victim I painfully lower myself into the driver's seat. Every bit of discomfort worth the inevitable outcome...FREEDOM!

The keys are tightly clasped in my right hand, bound in place by a sling. Like a horse chomping at the bit, I fumble for the keys in anticipation of the feeling that I'm so in need of, the feeling of independence. To be the woman I had once been if only for a fleeting moment. I put the key in the ignition and crank the engine. Thank god for automatics. I back out of the drive way with no destination in mind. My destination is not important, only the fact, that I can choose it.

OKAY

I wake up at 5:46 a.m. and as I wrestle with the pain I think of yesterday's brief escape from reality. It started as an excursion down memory lane as I drove past Bowdish Jr. High School where I first played basketball on a team and then passed by my old high school. But my flight of freedom ended with a glimpse into the future as I drove past lost memories, and shed tears for the places I would never share with Mark.

I tuck a pillow under my arm and close my eyes. My arm throbs but I don't feel it, not really. Instead the pain simply intensifies the pain in my heart until I cry and move on to my next task. It's my daily routine. Pain, cry, move ahead. Pain, cry, move ahead. It begins in the morning and repeats itself throughout the day.

When I crawl out of bed at 8:00 a.m., I shuffle to the kitchen with my cane and take something for the pain. Wishing I was wearing my sling to cradle my arm this morning, I rest my hand in my lap and bite back tears. I use my left hand to bring a spoonful of oatmeal to my lips. I can't wait to be where it's warm, to where the pain won't be so strong. At least I hope. And to where I won't be treated like a child. In two days I will be flying to Palm Springs to visit Honey and Bampa. I look forward to the change.

Today, however, I have an appointment with my attorney. Immediately following the accident, Northern Pacific Insurance, the company Mark worked for, and the company that insured Mark's car, had come to my parents and said, "Don't worry about a thing, just sign here and we'll take care of everything." My parents had decided that with everything they were going through, possibly losing their daughter and losing Mark, they would wait to sign any papers. The insurance company disappeared and didn't pay a dime. I now have an attorney. Kevin Milner came recommended by a friend of the family. We've met a few times but for now he is gathering information, while I gather debt.

After my appointment with Kevin, Dad drives me to physical therapy. I leave therapy with a new cane, one without four prongs at the bottom. I still hobble; I just look more stylish doing it. We stop at the shop, where Mom meets us for Reuben sandwiches. After lunch Dad drives me twenty miles home then returns to the shop. I settle into Dad's La-Z-Boy, drop my cane and cry. With my eyes closed, I see Mark. I see him on the court. I see him glancing in my direction as he sprints down the court on defense. I want him back.

I stay in Dad's chair until the tears are all gone. And when I open my eyes, I reach for one of the grief books on the side-table. I don't open it. I don't need to, I remember the important things. I hold the book to my chest with my left hand and close my eyes. The book recommends looking for support groups. I'm not sure I want support but after a long pause, I set the book down, reach for my cane and head to the kitchen drawer for the phone book. After several phone calls, I'm left with a number for hospice; they have a widow's support group. I call and leave a message.

Back in the living room I rummage through dozens of

video tapes Mom has pulled from her office. The National AAU tournament – Notre Dame. EWU vs. Montana. EWU vs. Gonzaga. I grab the Montana game and stick it into the VCR. Then it's back to the La-Z-boy. There's a jump ball and play begins. I bite my lip as I watch my teammates from the past run up and down the court. A tiny smirk creeps into my face. Man, those were ugly uniforms. I had always been thankful that, even though I hated the way I looked in red, our uniforms were not mustard brown like the University of Montana's. My eyes narrow as the tape continues to play. I watch my lean body run up and down the court, crashing boards, hustling on defense, and at first it feels good. But soon I'm missing what I will never again be apart of. Not college ball, but basketball. Basketball makes me feel whole. It makes life worth living and that part of me is gone along with Mark.

I turn off the VCR, the TV is still running but I no longer watch it. I don't move until there is a knock at the front door. There are two packages, both for me. The first is from SoloFlex. News of my accident has spread. The second is from Kirsten. I open the one from Kirsten. When I pull back the card board flaps of the box all I can see are empty candy wrappers. That's my Kirsten. I dig deeper; some of the wrappers have candy still intact. I pop a Hershey kiss in my mouth. As the chocolate melts, I scavenge through the wrappers and find, a book of word search puzzles, a hand painted journal, a plastic toy that looks like it came from McDonalds and the book Curious George Goes to the Hospital. I leaf through the book with what might be my first real smile since the accident.

When the phone rings, I reach for my cane and start the journey to the kitchen. The phone call is from Hospice. Yes, they have a support group that meets Thursday evenings at 5:30. The group runs in age, from 58 to 80 years old. I thank the woman and hang up the phone. I'm 25; I won't be attending the support group.

Eastern is having an alumni women's basketball game, one I am supposed to have played in, so we drive half an hour to my old stomping ground at Hec-Ed Pavilion. During college I would occasionally sit in the stands to watch men's games but I spent most of my time at Eastern on the court, so it's killing me to come as a spectator. And as I make my way with my cane through the stands, I feel as if I stick out. My hair is in a smooth ponytail (with Mom's help), and my clothes are basic college attire, but the way my body moves—the way my foot drags along with the cane, the way my arm hangs limp at my side— draws unwanted attention as I find my seat behind the bench. Poor girl, she's had a stroke. But in time I relax and watch the flow of the game, and my anxiety subsides. Basketball takes my mind away from daily life to the hardwood floor. The squeak of the shoes and the bouncing ball hypnotizes me, and transports me, at least for a short while, to a place and time without pain.

When the game is over Mom takes my arm and we make our way through the stands, only to be stopped by old coaches and players as we head to the door. One by one, they ask, "How are you doing?"

No one wants the truth.

"Good," I answer, "good."

Putz picks me up for my doctor appointments. The first is with Dr. Cooper, a plastic surgeon. His news is not comforting. I will need to wait a year after the last surgery (I have another in 14 months to remove a rod and pins) to consider any reconstructive work and he is not sure how much it will help. I'm not surprised and hope for better news from Dr. Perry, my orthopedic surgeon. I've been working hard and hope it will make a difference.

Putz sits quietly on the chair and I get up onto the padded table.

"Last time I saw Dr. Perry, he was covered in blood," Putz remembers.

"Nice," I say, remembering the account of the details. "I think you'll be safe this time."

There is a knock at the door and it opens slowly. Dr. Perry peaks in.

"Hi Sonya," he says, stepping in, file in hand. "It's good to see you."

I think he honestly means it and I feel the same. This man saved my life.

"You may remember my brother, Putz," I say, "He had to drive me since I'm not supposed to drive," I pause and raise my eyes brows, "yet."

Somehow my dad had known that I'd taken the car last week. And I'd been grounded for only the second time in my life.

"Hi," he says, ignoring my comment and reaching his hand to my brother's.

"How'd the X-rays look?" I ask.

"Well, the leg looks really good," he says. "The bone is healing well." He walks over and gently touches my shoulder. "Can you show me again how high you can lift your arm?"

I lift my arm 45 degrees away from my body and then Dr. Perry moves it around a bit more. I grit my teeth.

"I'm worried about your arm," he says. "I'd hoped you would have better range of motion by now."

Dr. Perry moves the arm around more and as he does my mind moves elsewhere. I've been working hard, harder than most, I'm sure. Maybe I've been pushing too hard. Maybe it doesn't matter. It doesn't matter. Nothing matters. What does it matter if I can't move my arm? I can't play basketball and I don't have Mark. Life doesn't matter.

Dr. Perry glances at Putz, then back to me.

"How are you doing?" he asks.

Four simple words. A simple question that I can't answer, instead I find myself holding back tears. I try to stop them but I can't. Dr. Perry rests his hand on my arm and allows me the time I need. With my eyes closed, I take a long slow breath. How am I really doing?

I have a 7 a.m. flight. Waking in time is easy for me. After a quick bowl of oatmeal and a long hug from Mom, Dad and I head out the door. Dad tosses my bag in the car, while I maneuver into the car without dropping my cane. Before Dad can close the door, I lean out across my body with my left arm and pull the door shut. Mom, gives me one last kiss through the open window then steps back onto the front door step, her long turquoise robe moving with the wave of her hand.

It seems like a long flight to Palm Springs. Though my body feels okay, I watch the clouds drift by and can't stop crying. No matter how hard I try to stop, tears keep coming. It seems as if it's all I ever do—cry. But I can't help it, even now, especially now. It seem as if the more time that goes by, the more I miss Mark and the more the reality of his death rips at my heart. It's not until I carefully lower myself down the plane's steep metal staircase, that my tears are gone. When a wheelchair, with my name on it, is at the bottom of the stairs, I nearly decline, but my cane makes it obvious it's for me, so I say hello and bum a ride to the arrival gate where Honey and Bampa are waiting.

I'm quick to stand and wrap my arms around them one at a time, first Honey, then Bampa.

"It's so good to see you" I say, starting again with the hugs.

"You look great," Honey says, reaching to my shoulder, "how are you feeling?"

"Better now." I say.

And I mean it.

I begin a two-week schedule that consists of sleeping and crying of course, but more importantly, talking, walking, eating, exercising in the pool, playing cards and watching the Los Angeles Lakers with Honey and Bampa. This new routine, along with the sun, helps lessen the pain, or at least change it a little.

A friend of Honey's, Solvig, whose husband died eight years prior, comes to sit with me in the hot tub and talks with me about being widowed. She's honest. She explains that living with Mark's death will be hard; dealing with my grief will be harder. She says it will be very difficult for the friends that Mark and I had known as a couple, and warns that I will become very lonely (I already know). But she promises that over time, it will get easier. I try to believe her.

It's Super Bowl Sunday. The name is enough to ruin my day. Mark would have been so excited. He loved big games. I once watched him fly across a TV room and pile on a couch full of innocent spectators in celebration of a Husky touch down. I can't handle the Super Bowl today so I'm glad we are going to a polo match instead. Still, once at the match, I feel awkward and out of place. Though I've made myself presentable, I sense eyes on me as I shuffle to my table with my cane. And since I'm not on a runway or shooting a jumper, I don't like it. I don't like the pity. I can pity myself, but damn it, no one else can.

After a couple of glasses of wine with Honey and Bampa, I relax and actually enjoy my first polo match. It helps that I love horses and that I can appreciate the athletic polo ponies and their riders. But as the day progresses, I'm eager to go home and lay down as pain creeps into my back and vertigo sets in, both of which have been getting worse over the past couple of days. Lowering my pain killers and upping my workouts have come at a price.

Two weeks pass. I continue to workout. And the pool rehab begins to pay off. I've increased mobility and I have reduced my painkillers to boot. But most of all, my spirits are lifted if only temporarily. There's a sad calm to Bampa as he drives past The Cliff House, now our favorite restaurant, on our way to the airport. Honey and I are barely holding back tears, but we keep them for our final goodbye, which will be accompanied by many hugs, before I board the plane. Time in the sun, away from my parents, was just what I needed, but now I'm ready to go home. If only I knew where home really was.

DESPERATE MEASURES

I've been living with my parents for five months. The gritty snow that's lined the sidewalks off and on throughout the winter has melted and makes it easier for me to get around. Because I've focused on rehab I'm able to walk smoothly with my cane and I'm finally allowed to drive which makes it easier for me and my family, when it comes to getting to my appointments. Driving would make it easier for me to get out and see friends too, but I have none in Spokane. I haven't lived here for years. It would make it easier for me to simply do things, but there is nothing I want to do, so I just keep moving through life. I go to doctor appointments and physical therapy. I join a gym to pick up the pace of my healing. I work for my dad entering 1991 tax data for Alpine Deli. I meet my parents at the shop for lunch and I watch a lot of TV. Pain is still a constant reminder of my fate, and every day is a struggle as I walk through life in a fog. I long for Mark and ache for freedom deep in my soul.

One day, when I'm plonked on the couch watching TV, the phone rings. It's Carol at Nordstrom's Fashion office in Seattle calling to see if I might like to come to Seattle for a week to help her and Helen with Nordstrom's upcoming SRO Spring

Fashion Show. My heart says, "Yes, go." My parents are not so sure. I call Carol the next day and take her up on her offer. That very same day Betty, my booker at Seattle Models Guild, calls to tell me she and Lynn have arranged for me to work in the fashion office at I. Magnin's as well.

"Would you like to work more?" Betty asks. "Modeling, I mean."

"I'd love to," I admit, "but I limp, I can't move my right arm much, and I've got really bad scars."

It seems so ridiculous I laugh to keep from crying.

"Get yourself back to Seattle and I'll get you work," Betty says.

I hang up the phone and plan my trip to Seattle.

The Overholts welcome me into their house during my trip to Seattle. They even line up a gym for me to continue my workouts. Since I have no money and in fact would soon have to pay taxes, I borrow money from my parents for a plane ticket and a rental car. I plan to pay them back, if only partially, with the money I will make. They will have nothing to do with it and pay for my visit.

When I pack my bags for the flight my heart is pounding. Mom helps find my nice clothes, which have been packed away. I've been living in pajamas and sweats. I will be able to wear flats or a very low heel and still be okay with my cane. The biggest problem will be making myself presentable for work, styling my hair. Moving my arm near the right side of my head is still very difficult. But since I'm not going to be on the runway, will just be in the back office pulling clothes and making phone calls, I decide my hair will be fine. I just hope I will. While driving the rental car to Mark's parents' in Everett, memories flood my mind, drowning my heart. I see Mark and me pulling up to the same house with his boat and a bucket full of fresh-caught crab. I see the entire family gathering around the table enjoying dinner. I hear the stories, the boat trips to the San Juans, the crabbing, the baseball games. They are a family built around togetherness and love. They've lost a part of their family. I'm reminded that I am not the only one hurting. Mark's loss seems even more senseless.

After arriving, Joan shows me to the guest room in the basement of their split-level house. I rummage through my old white suitcase, the one with "C" and "S" on the metal latches (Initials of my mom's maiden name). In the side pocket is a small folding frame that I remove and set on the bedside table and take a deep breath.

In the hallway there's a photo with Mark and his family. He looks so alive and leans into his youngest sister, a protector and friend. Mark loved this place, loved his family. Mark's sisters no longer live here, but just like Mark they are here in the walls, in every corner of this house. Wendy and her husband just moved to Everett. Vikki, whose wedding was where Mark had planned to propose, was now pregnant and expecting a baby soon and Debbie had recently moved to Seattle and started a new job. When Joan explains she's invited the girls for dinner later in the week, my shoulders tighten. I'm afraid, unsure of what I'll say when I'm with them, yet I want to know them better. To know Mark better.

Larry and I sit in the living room with Oscar Peterson jamming the keyboards in the background. I'm on the same couch where Mark once complained to me about a friend's choice, which bordered on infidelity, at a bachelor party. I loved him for that, for the passion of his morals on faithfulness. Larry's sitting by the fireplace, the fire is burning out. It's not easy for either of us, knowing if we talk about Mark, tears are inevitable. We had stopped by Mark's grave earlier in the day and it doesn't seem right to leave our thoughts about him unspoken, ignoring a life that was so meaningful to us both.

So one by one we share stories, and it feels good. But with joy comes pain, bringing finality to something, someone that should still be here. And for me, there is a feeling of guilt, of me being the reason for Mark crossing those tracks. Had it not been for me, had it not been for our love, our wedding, our bridal shower, Mark would still be alive.

Larry is quiet for a moment then swallows hard.

"Mark knew right away," he says, eyes now smiling, his mind drifting back in time. "He came home one night, came galloping up those stairs and said, 'Dad, I found myself a keeper!'" Larry sets his hands on his thighs and glances at the thick beige carpet before looking me in the eye: "Yep, he knew you were the one."

I bite my lip and then force a smile. There's nothing for me to say but I'm thankful Larry shared this with me. I had known too. I had tried to deny it at first, but I had known that Mark was the one for me. I had also known that we would always be together. My lips begin to tremble. I get up and hug Larry goodnight before my sadness escapes. Once in my room I sit on the bed and pick up the picture of Mark. In the photo I'm sitting in Mark's lap, arms wrapped around his neck. We're both wearing green baseball jerseys and blue caps that darken our faces in the shot. I hold the frame, hold Mark, tight to my chest and close my eyes. Always together, always. How could I have been so wrong?

Working in the fashion office at Nordstrom, I learn about the other side of my job. I call agents to hire models, label clothes that have been pulled for the show, and do a lot of paperwork. There is a lot to take care of before the show. There will be a rehearsal the morning of the show and today we're holding a fitting, a meeting where models try on the outfits and accessories that they'll wear in the show. It's comforting to have many of my friends around me, but it also emphasizes what I am no longer: a model. There are many new young faces. All thin, all graceful in their stiletto heels, all smiles. For once in my life I'm rail thin, but instead of being slim and graceful I feel like a beaten and starving child. I fade into the background, my heart and mind returning to Mark.

During the rehearsal at the Sheraton, I work backstage with the dressers and ready the models' clothes, shoes and accessories. During the show, I'm backstage as well. It's difficult to watch everyone fly around the dressing room, changing their outfits and tossing their hair into different styles, knowing that that part of my life is gone. As the models don their evening gowns and parade down the catwalk for the finale, I think of a time not so long ago when I was in this same room running backstage to change into a platinum blonde wig. With the wig came false eye lashes, red lips, a black dress and pumps that transformed me on the spot to Marilyn Monroe. I opened the scene lip-syncing "Happy Birthday" to a raspy, sexy Marilyn. Now as the models file off the stage, one by one, from their last strut down the runway, the reality of my life sinks deeper into my soul.

I wave goodbye to Grace and Kelle, and then return to the gold pumps, and other shoes, that I'm organizing for their return to Nordstrom. Lowering myself to the floor, I set my cane to the side and park myself on the short dark carpet, weight shifted to my left hip. I check for two shoes inside each shoe box and make sure they've been properly packed; heel to toe with tissue between. Then I remove the model name tags and load them into a larger box to be hauled to the store. Moments ago it was a frenzy of models pulling off jackets and pumps while running to their racks, now it's silent. The silence drives home the fact that I'm alone. Even worse, I'm alone on an important anniversary, the day Mark asked me on our first date. Fortunately I have plans for the evening; I'm going to a basketball game.

I used to coach girls' basketball at Blanchet High School with head coach Terry Wilkinson. I was Terry's assistant coach and the junior varsity coach. We had great teams, Varsity placed in State and my JV team was undefeated, but more important we had a lot of fun together. Terry and I became close friends discussing practice plans and games, and the ups and downs of life, at the gym and over pitchers of Rainer at the Lion's Den Tavern. I look forward to seeing Terry and his wife Marilyn and having the chance to watch the Braves, the team that dedicated their season to my recovery. I also look forward to having a chance to escape to a gym and the rhythm of my favorite game, basketball.

The gym's packed. Green and gold fill every breathable space. Electricity sparks the air. I'm surprisingly tense. Fearful of a sudden move, a rowdy fan doing what I love best as a player, jumping up and hollering, losing all sanity for a split second or an entire game. But I'm a bystander now, a weary and battered bystander. The crowd is almost too much, but with Marilyn's soft voice to hold me there, with the warm blessings of Father Doug, the priest who was to marry Mark and me, to hold me there, and the girls, the basketball girls, to hold me there, I stay. But I'm thankful when the game's over and the crowd's dispersed. With cane in hand, I move to the bottom step of the bleachers and stand in the vacant gym, waiting to congratulate Terry, coach Wilks, and to receive what I have unknowingly come for, his big hug.

Terry knows my pain, he and Marilyn both know it. The first year I coached with Terry, when I was just out of college, I listened with a young and untrained ear while the six foot-five-man shared not only his knowledge of basketball but his struggles with loss and grief. I saw how death brought hardship and suffering. Not only did he give me the opportunity to grow as a coach, he gave me the opportunity to grow as a person. While recovering at my parent's house in Spokane, I had received letters on a regular basis from Terry and Marilyn and colorful pictures from their kids. They knew what was important during a time of loss and because of that, during the game, Marilyn had given me an article about a Young Widows Support Group in Seattle.

"I don't know much about the group," she'd said, handing me a folded-up section of the Seattle Times, "but I thought it might be worth checking out."

"Thanks."

Questioning if I would make the effort to read the article, I had slid the paper into my coat pocket destined to remain there until it found its way to the garbage. Or perhaps some day I would find a need for it. But for now I wish Terry and Marilyn a good night, knowing I will survive one more day.

A black sky hangs over the cemetery. I pull on to the drive and stop as uncontrolled sobs blur my vision and shake my hands until I no longer have control of the steering wheel. I've visited Mark's gravesite twice with Larry, but tonight I'm alone. Sonia roses sit in the passenger seat next to me. "They'll just die," I tell myself as I reach across my body with my left hand to pick them up, "Why do I buy them? Why do I write on the stupid note card? It's not for Mark, it's for me."

I read the card to myself.

"Mark, I don't know if I can make it without you, it's so hard. I love you so much, what is life without you here? I miss you OV!!! Forever in love, Sonya."

I take the card off the flowers and tuck it into the rental car's ashtray before I set my cane outside the car and get out. There's a light-post not far from Mark's gravesite, and from the car I see that his grave is covered with flowers. Mark was loved, I think to myself, squeezing my eyes shut. Mark is loved. I open my eyes wide and blink, then lift my stiff body slowly out of the car and grab my cane. Vertigo has been bad today. I wait for my brain to stop moving before I walk with my cane over to Mark's grave. I stand, surveying all the flowers, white carnations, red roses, lavender flowers the name of which I can't remember, and more. I lower myself to the ground and since I can't kneel, after I place the bouquet of salmon pink roses next to some red carnations, I sit down and wrap my hands around my knees. For the longest time there is nothing. No words. No tears. Nothing. The tears are all gone. I just stare. This is not happening. This has not happened. Then I lower my head to my knees and weep.

The flight home to Spokane isn't easy, emotions stir as the clouds roll by; still after my visit I want to move back to Seattle more than ever. Once in Spokane, I search out a small news shop, purchase a Seattle Times and shoot straight to the classifieds. It's time to find an apartment manager position. It's the only way I can afford to move back to Seattle. With Betty getting me another week of work in I. Magnin's fashion office, I will have a start. I have no savings and recently called Honey and Bampa to borrow money, on the sly from my parents, to pay $2000 in taxes to the IRS. A loan I plan on repaying one day. Being an apartment manager would give me the opportunity to gain independence. With the inevitable onslaught of medical bills things could get scary, but I think with no rent or utilities I could manage. I'll take any job, push papers in a cramped cubicle all day, if Betty can't get me work modeling. I just need to be on my own again. There are three ads for apartment manager positions that fit my needs; a free apartment for the manager and less than 30 units in the complex. I drive back to my parents' house and pull out a bright yellow notepad and jot notes for my cover letter and a resumé. It doesn't take long because Mark and I had written a resumé for our job as managers just six months earlier. Once finished, I call each management position and gather information for my trip to Seattle the following week.

I have a lot to get ready before my trip, but it's difficult to get things done when I'm dizzy all the time, so Mom schedules an appointment with Dr. Benson, a neurologist. I also have a check up with Dr. Perry. Dr. Perry's appointment is first, and though he's happy with how my leg and arm are doing, he is concerned about my increased back pain which seems to be causing my limbs to go numb and is perhaps affecting my vertigo. A herniated disc is found to be the cause. The solution— more physical therapy. The appointment with the neurologist is next. It starts the same way most doctor appointments start, slow, and the news is relatively uneventful. My concussion has caused minimal brain damage. I leave the appointment with a list of more exercises, these being for my brain.

I meet with my attorney Kevin before leaving for Seattle. Dad and Mom join me at his office. My first concern is my medical bills. Northern Pacific Insurance won't give information to my Blue Cross insurance, so no bills are getting paid. It will be my responsibility to contact the billing departments and set up a payment plan of some kind so the bills won't get sent to collections. Kevin will keep working on Northern Pacific, since I don't have much money. I'm certain that just my Lifebird helicopter flight, from Ritzville to Spokane, had cost a pretty penny, and I hadn't even enjoyed a view.

Kevin splays photos on the fake wood desk.

"We're going to need photos showing your injuries." he explains.

I glance at the desktop and notice crumpled red metal and a tire visible on the corner of one. I swallow hard.

Kevin explains that we have a lot of time before the lawsuit must be filed but we have to gather as much information as possible. There are questions of where the lawsuit will be filed, what we will ask for, what I am worth. What I am worth? I look at my cane that sits by my side. Not much. I glance back at the photo of the mangled Chevy Lumina. Not much at all without Mark. When I leave the attorneys office I'm drained.

Back in Seattle I stay with Mark's parents again and feel more at home. Joan and I go through what is left of Mark's things. Things that have been moved from our apartment in West Seattle back to their home. Mark's family have already searched for the things that are meaningful to them. I take Mark's University of Washington baseball duffle bag. I'm sure I can smell Mark when I lay next to it at night. I imagine him with me.

I wake up alone, except for the duffle and my cane. I pick up the cane and run my fingers along the cold metal. I'll leave my cane today. I drive to Seattle to I. Magnin's fashion office. It's time for their spring show and I'm helping prepare for it just as I had for Nordstrom. On my lunch break, I make my own preparations; I schedule an interview for an apartment management position with Gordon Hopwood at Phillips Management. The day before my interview, Betty calls with a two hour print booking for Lamont's department store for a spring newspaper layout that happens to be at the same time as my interview with Gordon. Desperate for money, I take the booking and dial Gordon to reschedule. After which, Betty calls back and gives me a print booking in the afternoon. I take the booking and call Gordon to reschedule the rescheduled interview. No luck. I set the phone down on the receiver and sigh. Then limping, without my cane, I grab my old green backpack, and head to the car for the long drive to Mark's parents'. Jostling through traffic that seems to have thickened in the six months since I've been gone, I think about what has transpired. The good news is that I am getting work modeling.

The bad news is that I need an apartment management position to survive on my own.

I pull into the parking garage, up the hill from the Factoria Mall and Lowmans, a models' haven for sweet deals on designer clothing. I pull my heavy leather model's bag, the one I picked up in Greece for a dime, across the driver's seat and head toward the elevator. Lamont's has been my bread and butter and I'm happy that they're willing to take a chance with me again, but it seems like forever since I've been here and I feel my stomach grow tense as I step through the elevator doors. When I enter the studio, I walk slowly to mask my limp and am relieved to find Jonette, Digene, and Kelle chatting and touching up their make up at the mirror.

"Hi guys."

"Sonya, I'm so glad you're here," Jonette says, coming over and giving me a hug.

Kelle and Digene are right behind her.

"Thanks," I say. "It's good to be here."

I wouldn't have been able to manage zippers and buttons up my back but I have friends here to help. And thanks to jokes by Jonette every few minutes, the pain in my hip doesn't seem as bad and I'm able to smile. I make it through the shoot, scars and all.

The next day (the day before I'm to return to Spokane) my situation calls for desperate measures and, without an invitation, I plant myself in the Phillips Management office. I'm sure that if I meet Gordon, I might have a chance to get an apartment management position. Sitting in the office, I run the fingers of my left hand across my bangs and behind my ear, then set my damp palm on my slacks and wait.

"Yes, Gordon is in the office and will meet with you," the brunette at the front desk informs me with a lift of her brow.

I'm eye to eye with Gordon. He seems leery yet appreciative of my persistence. I show him my resumé and explain my circumstances, telling him I have some experience as an apartment manager with Mark. We finish the interview in the office, and then tour a 22-unit complex on Capital Hill. It's less than perfect, but when Gordon offers me the job, it's somehow perfect just the same. Bellevue Manor will be my new home and my new path to freedom.

PART IV
May 1992 — Seattle, Washington

REALITY CHECK

After living at Bellevue Manor for just one month, I've had a knife pulled on me, met a budding rock star, received several complaints of a tenant exposing himself, called the police twice, and learned more than I ever wanted to know about tattoos and body piercings. However, amongst all the chaos it's nice to be able to blend into the woodwork. Living on the first floor near the front door, I simply slip in and disappear into my hidden sanctuary to be alone with my sorrow.

Bellevue Manor is squeezed between two tall apartment buildings on the east side of Bellevue Avenue on Capital Hill. When I walk two blocks east to Broadway for groceries, I'm mildly entertained by the crowd. Men in drag who could strut the catwalk better than me (when I had a good leg), men and women I can smell from a block away sporting long dreadlocks and tattered jeans, and dozens of pale-skinned kids dressed in black who barely open their empty eyes. Most afternoons I wander north, on the oak-lined sidewalk of Bellevue Avenue for some exercise. If I walk far enough and get to the streets adorned with lavish brick Tudors and old Victorian mansions, I stroll in a more leisurely way, pretending for a moment that I live a different life.

Bellevue Manor is concrete and rock, and except for a 4'x 4' patch of grass, the landscape is concrete as well. This concrete leads into four parking spaces under the building. One of the spaces holds my red 85 Volkswagen Scirocco, Wolfsburg edition. I wheeled and dealed for the thing myself and managed to take out a loan in my name only, though I was 22 and self-employed at the time. It is my baby and it drives like a dream, if you have two good arms. The stick-shift is a struggle for me these days, but at least I can drive. And I'm fortunate to have a parking spot in the complex otherwise I'd have to search for street parking. Now I just park, pull myself up and out of the Scirocco with my good arm, ignore the stench of urine in the parking area, and walk by two cars to the front door.

If I were to look up before I stepped through the front door, I would see dirty cream-colored rock panels four stories high. But when I sneak in the front door, I only notice the rough brown rocks that jut out by the elevator and mailboxes in the lobby entrance. I had grandiose ideas of cleaning the place up, making it a nicer home. Cleaning the lobby, cleaning and painting the outside of the building and the stairwells, painting the brown rock wall white and adding flowers to the courtyard, like the villas in Greece, the villas I had hoped to share with Mark on our honeymoon. The villas where we would have held hands and made love. But all I've managed to do is plant peach geraniums, the kind that are always on Honey and Bampa's front porch. Flowers are as far as I have gone with Bellevue Manor and somehow I know it's as far as I will go, because the excitement of moving, of having my own place again has worn off. I have little energy to move ahead, to find tenants, to find a therapist, to live life. But I try. I have to. As an athlete I've learned to never give up. So I move forward and when I reach my limit and my energy is spent, I stop and I cry. And then I remember that Mark wants me to go on. So for him, I go on.

My one bedroom apartment on the bottom floor is a dungeon. Fortunately, the sliding glass doors from the patio allow some filtered light to sneak between the tall buildings and into my living room. With help from Mark's parents, who had been storing my furniture since the accident, I manage to get my furniture arranged. The cream love seat faces a small white entertainment center with an old TV with rabbit ears, a square glass vase filled with drooping yellow tulips, and a variety of wooden frames with pictures of Mark and me.

I have an old black chair that has followed me since Mom and I refinished it for my college apartment and a wobbly kitchen table with chairs. The small room is filled, but something's missing; without Mark it seems empty, just like my life. My life is a contradiction. I act happy; I feel sad. I want to live; I wish I were dead. My life is a lie. To keep my body and mind moving forward, I live the lie hoping it will one day become reality.

Today reality means bills. My mailbox is full of them. In just four weeks the walk to the mailbox has become a dreaded part of life. There are occasional letters from family, including a pink envelope from Honey and Bampa that arrives twice a week like clockwork. But the majority are bills asking for money I don't have.

With help from my bookers Betty and Lynn, I begin modeling right away. The Bon Marché and Lamont's department stores both book me several times, and on one occasion for lingerie, which pays time and a half. Both clients know I have scars but they work around them. My scars are proof of my strength to survive, at least physically but they are also a reminder of a life that will never be. My scars have become a part of who I am. But at work, even with an understanding client, they're a problem. I use makeup to lighten them, but I still have to I keep the right side of my body

141

away from the camera and discreetly cover the scars with my hand. Since I can't raise my right arm above my shoulder, it's difficult to change clothes, especially tight dresses and tops that go over my head. It's also hard to put a lot of weight on my right leg, which is the leg I have to lean on to keep my scars away from the camera. I do the best that I can. I need the work and, in this cut-throat and fickle industry of modeling, I'm lucky to be given a second chance. The hardest part of work is smiling. I can smile, I'm used to that. But each smile is a lie, a lie that becomes reality on a page and each smile is killing me inside.

To keep my sanity I visit the gym every night. I can now dribble the basketball and I'm able to shoot the ball with my left hand. I'm not very good with my left hand; but I never have been. I try to do yoga but my body is out of balance. The entire right side is weak and has minimal range of motion. Any pretzel-like moves are out of the question and even simple balance or stretching poses are difficult, not to mention painful. That is why in my heart of hearts, I know I should do them. And occasionally I try, but I know about weight lifting and swimming which are good for my rehab too, so I stick with them and throw in a little basketball, because just holding the ball brings me comfort.

With bills arriving daily, I realize I'm going to need more money. Which means I need more work. Which means it's time for a new card. A card is a 5 x 8 composite with pictures and measurements, that my agency sends to clients to get me work. To make a new card I have to hire several photographers to take pictures, which takes time and, of course, money. I schedule my first shoot. The night before the shoot, I pick out a black scoop neck dress and a simple teal turtle-neck for my head shot. I hang them, and a few more outfits, next to the door and go to bed.

I feel Mark lying next to me, the warmth of his body

against mine. I turn and put my face near his and breathe in slowly allowing my mind to savor what it can. I don't want to leave, but I have to. I wish I could wake Mark up to say good-bye; instead I silently peel myself from the sheets and tiptoe across the room. Before I step out the door, I glance in Mark's direction one last time, then shut the door. The hall is dark. I want to go back to Mark, but for some reason I move further and further into darkness. Enya is singing. I listen to the music. It grows louder and louder until finally I realize I'm still lying in bed. My back is sticking to the sheets with sweat. I drag my feet out from the covers and sit at the edge of bed. I blink several times trying to really wake up, trying to blink the sleep out of my eyes, but it wouldn't go away and my eyes even sting. I walk to the bathroom and once in front of the mirror I realize I won't be getting new shots for my card today. For the first time in my life I have a sty in my eye. I cancel my shoot and crawl back into bed alone.

My journal is my savior. I write when the crying stops and I cry when the writing stops. They work together, crying and writing, to pull me through. In my journal I can bitch about life and no one looks away or worse, looks at me with pity. Today is a good day, and I'm grateful.

May, 1992

It's good to be back in Seattle. I've been doing my stretches and walking, but I'm looking forward to starting rehab here. I've started going to a health club and am checking out some physical therapists. My arm seems like it's gotten more range of motion, but it also hurts more. I'm getting used to the pain. My back is really stiff without receiving massage, so I'll

143

probably try to get a massage next week if I can...
The Overholts are great. After staying with them,
they helped me move. It was good to stay with them,
but also very hard, I'm sure for them as well. It's
been hard thinking about going on without Mark.
Sometimes it doesn't seem possible but I'm doing the
best that I can.

I MISS YOU, MARK!
Love Sonya

※

The sun warms my body despite the crisp breeze that sweeps off the rocky shore at Myrtle Edwards Park. Dad and I sit on a bench enjoying our bratwurst, like we have nearly every other Tuesday for the past three years. Twice a month he travels from Spokane to Seattle to pick up meat, bread, and wine for his shop, Alpine Deli. We have a routine that I treasure. One that I need now more than ever. Our bench, next to a path, faces the open water. I watch in envy as joggers pass by.

"Sometimes it all seems like a terrible nightmare," I finally manage, my voice fading into the Puget Sound.

Dad is quiet. He knows. He knows all too well. Except in his nightmare his daughter survives which makes for a better ending.

Now he is having another nightmare.

"I hope Uncle Kurt's going to be okay," I break the unusual silence again; Dad's mind is miles away with his brother in Austria.

I think back to the last time I saw Uncle Kurt. He, Tanta Maria, and cousin Kurti had welcomed me into their home in Haag am Hausruck, Austria. I had been modeling in Greece, and flew to Austria for a long weekend. I have photos from the visit. One is of Uncle Kurt and me walking Markt Platz in front

144

of Gasthaus Gaubinger and my favorite picture is one in which Uncle Kurt has his arm around me and we are both holding up our beer mugs. He seems so alive and now cancer is eating him up.

"How are you feeling?" Dad asks, putting his hand gently on my leg. I look up from his strong hand. His sandy-blonde hair has begun to grey. He is getting older. I've never really noticed it before. I think of Dad looking just like he did when I was young. But life ages everyone, and though he is still handsome, I see that life has aged him as well.

"Oh, I'm okay," I smile and look into his clear blue eyes.

He forces a smile, fighting back the tears I can't.

Giving me a long hug he then gathers our emptied paper sacks.

"I hope you have a good flight, Dad," I say, limping slightly as we make our way back to the car. "You should make it there in time, shouldn't you?"

"I hope so."

Easter, one year ago, I had known Mark was going to ask me to marry him and that I would become Mrs. Overholt. I was wrong; this Easter is proof of that. I'm spending Easter alone, crying. I only find relief in knowing I will not be disturbed.

The day after Easter my Uncle Kurt dies. Six days later I pick up Dad from the airport. We sit in his truck for a while and talk and cry. We cry for Mark, we cry for Uncle Kurt, and we cry for each other. Dad had made the hectic twenty-two hour flight to Austria and arrived right after his brother died. Dad and I share more than just our olive skin tone and tempers, we share the feeling of loss one feels from not being able to say goodbye.

Dad stays in Seattle so the next day we drive to Discovery Park and stroll through the woods. The trail, which I have run many times in the past, has a clearing high on the sand dunes overlooking the Sound. It's a breathtaking view, and with Dad by my side, I'm inspired. I realize I need a new goal in my life. If I can't have Mark, I want back the other most important part of my life. I want to play basketball again. In silence I reach for Dad's hand. I know I will suffer the next day from the long walk, but it was worth it. Every step was worth it.

THAT GIRL

I find a physical therapist. I follow several recommendations, which all lead me to Philip. Philip evaluates my injuries and establishes a plan. There is little hope that I will regain full flexibility and function of my arm, but I figure if I can get my arm strong enough to move without pain, then maybe I can rebound and shoot left-handed in a game. I let Philip know I'm an athlete and I will do the exercises he recommends. I need to get better. He puts me to work. It's painful, but I can feel the exercises and stretches working within a week. With my goal to play basketball again, I know I can handle the pain.

Massages are an important part of my recovery. They help relieve the constant pain and help to slowly increase flexibility I have lost from my injuries. But more importantly, my massage therapist Monica, who is an old friend and teammate of mine from college, puts up with my constant banter. Moon, as I have called her since our days on the court at Eastern, is a counselor of sorts for me (who happened to go to high school with Mark). Our times together are times of healing. It doesn't hurt that she gives me a discount, since my insurance doesn't cover massage and the money comes right out of my shallow pocket so I promise myself I will pay her back someday.

147

Receiving a lot of massage peaks my interest in it. I've always enjoyed giving a massage, but now I see the importance of its healing powers. I explore going to massage school. I struggle with the reality of the commitment. Maybe it's because of a deep-lying need to heal or perhaps simply a way to distract me from my grief while focusing on the physical aspect of healing, but whatever the reason, I decide to try. I interview at Brian Utting School of Massage and sign up for a workshop to see if I can physically handle giving a massage.

I'm not sure how I will pay for school since money is tight. But I'm hoping to receive some lost wages from the insurance claim connected to the accident. I know I can't count on it, but I also know I'll figure something out if the insurance money doesn't come through. Work? My Visa card? A loan? I will find a way.

At the workshop I show the instructor that my body can handle giving a massage, but because of my circumstances, because of losing Mark, I'm required to meet with a counselor. I meet with the counselor and then return for a final interview. The woman who gives me the final interview seems skeptical, but she doesn't know me. She doesn't know what I'm capable of. I've been hit by a train and survived. Having to pull myself up the two steep flights of stairs, one step at a time, to get to her desk on the second floor, is nothing. I could do it again and again to come to class, and each time it would get easier. I want to lean on her desk now and let her know I'll be back. A week later I hang up the phone and let the good news swim around in my head while I make myself a cup of peppermint tea. I will attend the Brian Utting School of Massage in the fall.

As I set down the letter from the attorney's office my hands begin to tremble. Why do I have to deal with this? Isn't losing Mark bad enough? The letter informs me that my attorney can no longer work on my case. After the accident Mark's car

148

insurance had refused to make any payments. The attorney has been working on my case for almost seven months now. Our relationship, never great, has been rapidly deteriorating. I don't need a million dollars. I just need money to cover my medical bills. Had I been Mark's wife, I would have received his life insurance, but I was not Mark's wife and even that money would have only begun to pay my bills. I'm doing the best I can to keep myself out of collections. But I don't know how long I can keep it up. And now the possibility of getting help to pay for my medical bills through a lawsuit will be delayed until I locate a new attorney to take over my case.

May 1992

I'm second-guessing my decision to go to massage school. Maybe it will be too much. Today was such a terrible day, I didn't think I would make it. First thing this morning a water heater broke in apartment 13, which started leaking down into the next apartment. Fortunately I turned off the water and we got someone out to fix it right away. But then there was the rest of the clean-up and the wet carpets and walls. I didn't even want to deal with it. Good thing Pat, the handyman, could take care of most of it. Cleaning the lobby and vacuuming three flights of stairs was enough to do me in. I can't squat down so it's awkward reaching anything low. And just doing a little bit with my right arm makes it go numb. I hate this place. I wish this were all a big nightmare. I wish I would wake up and Mark would be lying next to me, his face nuzzled into mine. Please make this all be a nightmare. Please let me wake up. Please, Mark, please.

❄

Today I get to see Mark's mom, Joan. It's been a couple of weeks and I'm looking forward to it. I'm meeting her at a baseball game in Everett. Mark's old high-school team is playing. The ache I feel in the pit of my stomach is overwhelmed by the throbbing of my shoulder, but I still know it's there. My senses are heightened in this unfamiliar territory; Mark's high-school baseball and everyone who is associated with that time, people I don't know.

I slowly ascend the stairs of the large stadium where the game is being held. I find Joan and as people stand to let me by, I slip sideways along the bench and squeeze in by her side.

"I'm glad you could make it," she smiles, looking me in the eye.

"Thanks," I adjust to keep my weight on my left hip. "I'm glad you invited me."

"How's work?" Joan asks, eyes now on the game.

"Good." I answer, and then hesitate for a moment. "It's really nice to see you, Joan."

She rests her hand on my leg just briefly and gives me a soft smile before returning her focus to the game. "Number 5 is a great shortstop; he's also a starting guard on the basketball team. He's a real hustler." She pauses for a moment. "He reminds me of Mark."

We stand to let a woman squeeze by.

"Hi Joan," says the middle-aged woman with short dark hair, as she turns to look at Joan before sitting in her seat. "I'm so sorry about Mark."

"Thanks," is all Joan can manage.

"How's that girl doing?" the woman adds, and I feel the ache in the pit of my stomach sink deeper. In my mind I've left the stadium and I'm running as fast as I can. That Girl. People think of me as That Girl. Not Mark's fiancé, not Mark's girlfriend, and certainly not Mark's wife (that was 18 whole days away), but That Girl. I'm screaming at the top of my lungs, in my mind, while I pretend to focus on the game. I hold back tears as Joan introduces me to the woman, a teacher from Mark's old high school. I smile and manage my best "Nice to meet you" as I'm introduced as Mark's fiancé.

After the game, I drive onto I-5, just to turn off again and stop by Mark's grave. I stay there for two hours. And for two hours I cry. By the time I drive the half an hour home, I've stopped, but what little spirit I've gained as of late, has been broken. I'm certain I can't go on.

LONELY

The team bench is not a place I'm comfortable. I like to be on the court, on the field, in the game. But today the bench is okay. Greg Riz, the coach of the Seattle Models Guild softball team, the team I used to play on before my accident, insisted that I help coach. I couldn't say no. Wearing my assistant coach jersey, I sit on the bench and cheer. Softball games became a part of my life after meeting Mark. I followed him around to softball tournaments almost every weekend. I cheered as he stole bases and threw out runners. Yes, it's good to be here on a softball diamond, I just wish I were cheering for Mark.

"Maybe you can start playing a little," Greg says, scooting next to me on the bench.

"I can't throw the ball and I can't run, so it might be a problem," I say, laughing at the idea while it turns in my mind.

"Well, you could play first base. All you really have to do is catch," he says.

Greg grabs a bat and leaves the dugout. I watch him and wonder if maybe he's right.

The next day I talk to Mike Atwood. Mike was to be a groomsman in our wedding and was a softball teammate of

Mark's. I ask when the Rainier's, Mark's old team, will be having their next game. We decide to get patches made for their team uniforms in Mark's memory and agree on circular black patches for their sleeves, with the number 4 above OV, and a line dividing the two. The patch has a double meaning. 4 was Mark's number and OV was his nick name. The Rangers would be playing for Mark Overholt: 4 OV.

When I arrive at the Ranger's game with the patches and not Mark, my chest tightens. I've spent game after game chatting with the players, their girlfriends, wives, mothers and fathers, but I really didn't get to know them. Most of the time, I had been focused on Mark, thinking I would have the opportunity to get to know all of them better in the future. I was wrong.

I can't remember anyone's name. I recognize them all, but names escape me. Maybe the memory loss is due to post-traumatic stress disorder or perhaps because of the brain damage from my accident. I assume it is because I'm bad with names and I begin to wonder why I came to the game and put myself in this position. But as soon as I near the field, Mike comes over to say hello, along with a few other players. They reintroduce themselves and their significant others, they give me Mark's jersey and before long I'm sitting amongst them in the stands. I make conversation, but just as before my focus is on Mark. I look out to the field. I can see Mark fielding a ball, running the bases, winking in my direction from the batter's box. I can see it all as if he were here, alive. I continue to talk holding back the tears that will come once I'm alone.

When I get home I retreat to my quiet dungeon, like I do most nights. I sit on my loveseat with Brianna in my lap and stare at pictures of Mark. Because I make myself refill the vase each time the flowers wilt and die, bright tulips peer back at me, as well. And though having fresh flowers somehow helps me this evening, it would be better to have someone to talk to. Sometimes I call Kirsten, at any hour, day or night, and she listens until I change the direction in the conversation into trying to convince her to move back to Seattle. But most of the time I sit and weep. Tonight when I can't sit any longer, and the tears are all gone, I'll pay bills. And while I cower over the table and write checks, spending money I don't have, this life of mine, that can't possibly get worse, does.

Physical therapy gives me one thing to live for, the possibility of a body that works. I also enjoy Philip's company and I like to think he enjoys mine and enjoys having a patient who will do exercises at home. As an athlete I'm used to pushing my body, I'm used to a scheduled workout and now, literally, I live for it.

"Let's start you walking on the treadmill again today," Philip says as I follow him to the nearest machine. "How's your body doing?"

I step on to the rubber track and think about the weekend, the bouts of vertigo, the constant ache in my shoulder and hip and the sleepless nights from neck and back pain. Furrowing my brow, I scrutinize the treadmill's control panel.

"It's doing okay."

Walking to the softball diamond with my hand in a glove feels right. I look a bit silly sauntering up to the dugout for the Seattle Models Guild softball game, because I can't get the smile off my face. Today I'm going to play. I called Greg earlier in the week and took him up on his offer to get in the game and play first base. I explained, again, that I couldn't throw, but he didn't seem to care. And I'm glad.

We're up to bat first and fortunately I'm far down on the lineup, because butterflies are beginning to take up residence in my stomach. I watch as one by one my teammates get on base until I'm on deck. I take a deep breath, grab a bat and step out of the dugout. I just need to tap it down the third base line so I can have time to jog to first. I gently swing the bat, testing my range of motion. There's a pang in my shoulder but it isn't too bad. I swing a few more times until my shoulder rotates more smoothly and with less pain. If I can just get to first. Mary hits a single and then John hits a line drive double. There are more butterflies. I walk up to home plate and take a deep breath. Once I'm on first, I can have a teammate run the bases for me. Strike. I let the first pitch go by. Okay Sonya, whatever you do, don't go down watching. I dig my feet into the dirt and look up at the pitcher. My heart is soaring. To be here is heaven. To get a base hit…

As a kid I played fast pitch, so high pitches are tough for me to hit. When the pitcher releases the ball it makes it's way to the plate in a high arch. I try to be patient. Time slows. I watch the ball hit my moving bat and dribble toward the mound. I put my head down and run as fast as my bum leg will take me and somehow it gets me to first. It's not enough however, to get Mary to home plate. I should feel bad about the out, but I'm too excited that I've gotten to first base. Greg calls for a runner and as I walk to the bench my heart won't stop pounding. It feels so good to be playing, to be part of a team.

The Seattle Club is like my new home. It's clean, has a pool and most importantly it has a basketball court. Visiting the club is part of my routine, a routine that includes showing apartments, cleaning apartments, rehab, and occasionally modeling. I like to go to the gym late at night when the court is empty, and after a good hour of lifting and stretching, I step on to the basketball court to begin my comeback. Dribbling back and forth, back and forth, the rhythm of the ball works its magic on my body and soul. My mind focuses and I'm able to forget all that has gone wrong, if only for a moment.

Tonight as I dribble from end to end, my body wants more. I want more. Then as if lifting a boulder, I push the ball toward the basket and it falls short—way short. There is a stabbing pain in my shoulder. I decide to stick with dribbling. I need the safety. I need to know I can do something I used to do and love. I need to know that at least one small thing in my life hasn't changed. When I finally look at the clock, it's time to get going, in order to have time for a swim. Holding my ball near my face in some semblance of shooting position, I drink in the familiar smell of leather. Tears well in my eyes, but I go to get on my swimsuit before they fall.

I have always sunk like a rock in water and now with the right side of my body nearly immobile it's impossible to keep afloat without help. I tighten up my blue belt flotation device and start with a sidestroke. Maybe the blue will blend in with the water, making the belt invisible to those walking by. I swim my last lap and stop at the shallow end to finish with some exercises for my shoulder. With a half an hour until closing, I retreat to the jacuzzi to be alone. Once alone in the jacuzzi, I close my eyes and lower myself into the water. As the heat surrounds my body, I sink deeper until water grazes my chin. A mist drifts across my face as the water whisks away the tension in my body. Though I'm glad to be home, in Seattle, I feel more deeply the pain of all that is missing in my life. I am desperately lonely.

I thrive on independence. I have to; my life is solitary. My best friends live outside of Seattle and the rest of my friends are basketball players and models. And since work is sparse and I can't frequent my usual gyms, I rarely see any of them. And what would these friends say to me if we went to lunch? The conversation would not be easy. No one wants real answers. How's work? I'm not making enough to pay my bills and will soon be sent to collections, but at least I'm working. Too bad you can't play ball? They could never know how much it is killing me inside. Now more than ever I need to get on the court and release the anger and pain in my heart. How are you doing? How do you think I am doing?

Lowering myself to the floor, I push in the video tape of Mark's funeral. I lean against the loveseat and pull my knees into my chest as best I can. Holding the remote in my hand, I start to cry. I wait for a moment and imagine what the video might show before I push play.

I imagine the church as our church, the one we were to be married in, although I know it isn't. I imagine a tearful ex-girlfriend slipping into the role of the grieving widow as I lay helpless in my hospital bed. I imagine Mark's family moving slowly through a scene that is as foreign and unthinkable to me as it is to them. I imagine Larry and Joan working to make Mark's memorial service warm and welcoming for the people, many of whom I don't know, who have come to shed tears for their first born and only son.

There would be flowers. Sonia roses perhaps, draped over the casket. The church pews would be overflowing. People standing in the aisles. Friends and family would share stories of their love for Mark. Groomsman Chris, sporting a crew cut, would know what must be said. Mark's best man, Mickey, might feel lost, unsure of what to say, with that part of him gone. All of Mark's friends, who happened to be girls, would cry knowing they would never receive another hug or broad smile to warm their hearts. There were so many people who loved Mark, there was so much of our lives yet to be explored.

What would it have been like to walk up to the open casket and view Mark's lifeless body? His shining spirit, his endless energy gone. I imagine myself tentatively reaching out to sample the truth. To feel the coldness of his once supple skin. Would I have reached out to hold him and, desperately clinging to his cold body, need to be pried away? Or would I have gently kissed his cheek, let go and backed away silently as tears rolled down my solemn face?

I will never know.

I push play. I can hardly see the video through my already tearful and swollen eyes. It's hard to watch the funeral service, friends and family one by one emptying their hearts about Mark. I struggle to recognize people. How could I not have known all these people? Mark and I had been so wrapped up in our love for one another, we had forgotten about everything else. Or perhaps it was just me. My mind was focused on Mark. I was waiting until a later date to allow myself to open up and get to know Mark's friends. So much has been lost. When the memorial service ends, a video assembled by Mark's family runs. Pictures of Mark set to music tear at my heart. Each picture fills the screen with Mark's essence, each telling a different part of his life and doing it well. For the rest of my life, "Forever Young" and "Tears in Heaven" will bring tears to my eyes. I play the tape again and again and when my tears are finally gone and I go to bed, my heart is empty.

TURNING POINT

I miss Mark more than ever. I miss everything about him but most of all I miss his friendship. I need help. I pull out the article Marilyn gave me months ago about the young widows support group and then pick up the phone and dial.

I'm sweating as I pull into the church parking lot and my heartbeat quickens as I walk to the door. Wiping my palms on my faded jeans I turn the door handle and make my way down the carpeted hallway. Peering into room B, I see a circle of chairs. Several people, widows, are seated but most are milling around. Most are dressed in work clothes. All are much older than me.

I scoot quietly into a seat. It seems like a lifetime before the group gathers and one by one we introduce ourselves and explain how we became widows, or in my case became almost a widow, became a That Girl. I hold back tears with a quick swallow and, keeping to the point, let the next sad story fill the circle.

One by one stories of tragedy unfold. A 42-year-old woman's husband died in his sleep two years ago. A 32-year-old woman was left with three young children, her husband dying of cancer four and a half years ago. A 38-year-old man lost his wife to breast cancer last year. He is raising their daughter alone. Will I be this miserable three years from now? I can't feel this way for three more years. It's already been seven months and I can barely stand life any more. I feel sick inside. Mark wouldn't have wanted me to live like this. And I don't want to, either. I don't know how to make the pain go away but I do know I can't go on living like this. Though it is good to see that I'm not alone in my sorrow, I never return to the young widows support group and instead move forward with my life.

❋

After college I had purchased major medical for $46 a month so that my parents wouldn't have to help out if I broke my leg or blew out a knee on the court. I never dreamed I'd be hit by a train. The file I've made for my medical bills is now bursting. Many of the bills are from doctors I've never even heard of. I know all the major players in the game, my game of life, but there are so many I don't remember sometimes I call to see what a doctor did for me following the accident, and then with no way to prove them right or wrong. I pay the bill.

Sitting on the small folding chair I pull up to the kitchen table, I extend my right leg out long and move to take weight off my hip. The daunting pile of bills that I've collected over the past three days, stares at me, daring me to run to the couch and cover my head with a blanket. I think about it. I think about curling up and paying attention to my mind. To watch the movies that run there but are no longer as vivid as they once were. Movies of Mark and me, together, holding hands and touching lips, as young lovers do. Movies I will watch until they fade to black and white. Movies I will always watch alone, because I'm the only one who knows them.

Instead, I pick up the soft ivory envelope, with an embossed forest green logo I know well. The letter is from my attorney's office. Kevin has, in my eyes, been faltering in communication, even more so since he had informed me that he would no longer be able to represent me. This makes our interim relationship very stressful. Kevin recommended a replacement but my gut instinct told me not to go with him. So I've begun my own search for an attorney. I've seen five, thus far. One I verbally agreed to have take over my case and then after sleeping on it, changed my mind. All of this isn't going over well with Kevin and it's killing me. I'm hesitant to open the letter.

Dear Sonya:

As was explained to you, because of personal circumstances, I have been unable to continue with my current case load. I made arrangements for you to meet with attorney Luis Samuelson and Vince Trapetto. It was my hope that Vince Trapetto could substitute as counsel for you.

Luis and Vince advised me that after meeting with you for over two hours to fully discuss the status of your case and the potential of Vince Trapetto becoming your attorney. With your permission, I had your entire file copied and delivered to him in advance of that meeting. Vince and Luis informed me that you declined to be represented by Vince.

I have been advised by both Luis and Vince that you are considering retaining counsel in the Seattle area to represent you. He advised me that you intended to meet with other attorneys in the coming weeks and would let him know of your decision.

When I discussed my personal situation with you and your father, I did so in the sincere hope that we could make a smooth transition to another attorney. I hoped we could do so in a manner that would have no adverse effect on your case and assorted on you. I warned both you and your father of the danger of attorney, friends and other "know-it-alls" trying to take advantage of your situation for pecuniary gain or using their "knowledge" to puff their egos without having your interests as their main concern. I believe that is what is now happening to you, and I hope what I have to say below will stop that.

Luis Samuelson and I have both done a good job on your case. Despite what I have been advised that one attorney told you, we did file (and you signed) a claim with Adams County, Washington. Its claim representative has been in contact with both Luis and me. Your case would have been filed had you signed and returned the complaint to us.

Be careful of becoming so involved with obtaining advice from non-lawyers that they inadvertently cause you emotional harm and cause harm to the status of your case as well. Luis, Vince and I have years of experience in litigation. Be careful of letting your emotions cause you to accept well-meaning but harmful advice from those with no experience.

You should assist Luis and me in helping you retain an attorney who is qualified and able to give your case the energy and experience of a good attorney. Your delay in doing so is causing your case harm. It hurts me to see this happening. You must listen to those of us who sincerely have your best interests at heart.

I spoke with your father. He is a rational, calm and intelligent man. Call him, listen to him and follow his advice. Work with Luis and your father. They can help *you. At times like this, you need a support system based on love and concern, not greed or ego.*

I am formally withdrawing from representing you. I can no longer be responsible for your case. Please get control of the situation and let Luis or your father help you.

I sincerely wish I was able to assist you.

Unfortunately, I cannot. I wish you the very best and hope all goes well for you in the future.

Sincerely,
Kevin Melton

The first line is the best part of the letter, the only part that doesn't make my blood boil. The only part that doesn't make me want to scream bloody murder. I pick up the phone and dial.

"Mom, I just got a letter from my attorney," I feel my face getting red. "Kevin treats me like I'm a little kid, listen to this,"

I move to the couch and begin to read.

"First, the letter explains why he can't continue as my attorney, which is fine. He reminded me that he is having personal problems," I let out a short breath. "I am truly sorry he's having personal problems, but I've got a few right now, too."

"It'll be okay," Mom tries.

"Okay?" I roll my eyes. "You know the guy he recommended in Spokane? The guy with the slick black hair and dollar signs in his eyes? Kevin is mad I didn't pick him. He was probably supposed to get a kickback or something."

"Sonya," Mom gives me a halfhearted "Shame on you," only because she feels it's a mother's job to do so.

"And I'm still looking for someone over here that I feel like I can trust. It's not easy. I mean can you really trust any attorney?" I take a deep breath. "I don't need a lot of money. I just need to cover my bills, pay for my medical. I could never replace Mark with money, and since we weren't married, he can't even be brought up in court. What did they say, no punitive damages, something like that. It doesn't matter anyway, it won't bring him back."

Brianna's tail begins to twitch and I stop for a second to gently take her off my lap and set her on the floor, before I catch a second wind.

"And Mom, listen to this, he writes, 'I warned you and your father of the danger of attorneys, friends and other "know-it-alls" trying to take advantage of your situation for pecuniary gain or using their "knowledge" to puff their egos without having your interests as their main concern. I believe that is what is now happening to you, and I hope what I have to say below will stop that.' Who does he think he is? Shit, Mom, I'm an adult. He's one of them, he doesn't care about me or he would have explained that I needed to find a different attorney a long time ago."

I stand up and walk back to the table.

"He's trying to put all this on me, papers being filed late and stuff. Listen to this, 'Your case would have been filed had you signed and returned the complaint to us.'" I sit down and add, "thank god I didn't."

Mom listens patiently, then says, "I know this is frustrating, but it's going to be for the best. I've been talking to some attorneys at work to see if they can get any names for me."

"Mom, I'm so sick of this. How do you really know if an attorney is any good?" I ask. "All of them so far have seemed…" I raise my eyes and ponder. "I don't know, I just don't have a good feeling. I don't know what to do."

Looking at the letter, I think of the stress this whole process of finding an attorney has added to my already stressful life.

"Listen to the rest of this, 'Be careful of becoming so involved with obtaining advice from non-lawyers that they inadvertently cause you emotional harm and cause harm to the status of your case as well. Be careful of letting your emotions cause you to accept well-meaning but harmful advice from those with no experience.' Didn't he say the same thing twice? I mean, I'm smart enough to figure that out."

I'm on a roll and not even Mom can stop me.

"He even goes on to say it hurts him to see this happening to me. Right, it hurts his pocket book."

"Sonya, that's not true."

"Bullshit, Mom, you know this stupid thing is worth money," I fire back wishing we weren't talking about Mark's lost life this way. "I just want to find someone I can trust to take care of it, get it over, without all this bullshit."

I skip to the last couple of paragraphs to read what is really eating at me. "Listen to this. 'I spoke to your father.' Hello! I am a 25-year-old woman." I continue. "'He is a rational, calm and intelligent man.' Obviously, Kevin doesn't know Dad and I have the same temper."

Mom gives a courtesy laugh.

"'Call him, listen to him and follow his advice.' Does he know that Dad says I should do what I feel is right? Of course not." I take another breath, "There's more, 'Please get control of the situation and let your father help you,'" I read. "Can you believe it? And he even underlined the 'please.' Come on. Who's the one who needs to get a grip?"

After laughing at my own joke, I realize that I'm already feeling better.

"It'll be fine. He's just going through some hard times, let's forget about it as much as we can and move forward." The Ford collector business tone, from 10 years as a collector, moves into her voice for a brief moment before she continues, "Dad's coming to see you tomorrow. He should be there by lunch."

Arranging our Leberkase and Havarti sandwiches and apple juice on napkins in the center of the bench, Dad and I settle in for lunch at our favorite spot in Myrtle Edwards park. I fill Dad in on my life in Seattle. The modeling I've been doing. How difficult it's been to keep up with massage school homework but that the giving and receiving of massage has been helping me physically. And last, how I've recently decided that when I'm done with massage school, I'm going to travel to Europe. He of course loves the idea. After discussing where I should go and what I might do, I come back to a topic that has been haunting me, finding an attorney. Dad listens quietly, and agrees that I'm doing the right thing.

"It will take time, Sonya," he says, and reaches to hold my hand, "but you will find someone, someone you trust."

PART V
June 1992 — Seattle, Washington

HOPE

"You've gotta see this one kid who's on the highschool team I coach, he looks just like Mark," Mike had said. So with an aching heart and an open mind, I drive to the game. To once more be a part of the groomed diamonds, the crack of the bats and the smell of fresh-cut grass, baseball things that so remind me of Mark. After months of physical therapy I'm no longer mistaken for someone who's suffered a stroke. But I'm still suffering. The suffering I feel is the pain in my heart and the emptiness that follows me everywhere, emptiness that weighs on my soul like the ballast of crushed rocks that lay beneath my body the day of the accident. It's a painful weight that each day I dutifully drag from place to place. And today I feel that weight as I make my way to the bleachers and find a quiet seat.

I sink into the bench, remembering so many games where I'd cheered for Mark. Many times I'd wished I'd been alone so I could follow the game more closely. Today, I'm alone and I watch the innings pass with a contentment I hadn't expected. I remember Mark's love for the game and savor the intricacies that were so much a part of his life. It feels good to be out. It feels good just to feel again.

I scan the players looking for someone who resembles

Mark, but see no one. I'm surprised by my disappointment. I'd unexpectedly developed a desire to see this person, though I know it won't be like having Mark back, I scan the outfielders again. No luck. Just enjoy the game, I remind myself. I am deaf.

When the inning ends, the players jog off the field. Running toward the dugout the left fielder tilts his head up and flashes a smile to one of his teammates. There it is. Mark's smile on this 16-year-old kid! I can't believe it. Tears begin to fall. Mike was right: it's like seeing just a small piece of Mark and it's worth it.

I sit back and enjoy the game. The left fielder, the one that looks like Mark, catches a pop fly for the first out of the 4th inning. The next batter steps to the plate and takes a strong swing at the first pitch. Not fully connecting, the ball flies straight up and spins toward the backstop. The catcher whips around, throws his mask to the ground and looks up in search of the foul tip. He catches it, facing the crowd. I stare in surprise. The catcher looks just like an old friend from college, Jason Elliott.

I had seen Jason once after college, right before I left for Europe to model in the fall of 1989. I ran into him in Downtown Seattle. It was late at night and the conversation was short, but I left knowing he was working for Beecham and that he was as sweet as ever. I want to smile thinking of him now, but I know I shouldn't. Even thinking of another man is being disrespectful to Mark. When the catcher walks back to his dugout, I focus on the game.

A week passes. My apartment's now a safe haven from the sun as well as from life itself. As I clean apartments, attend massage school, search for an attorney, go to rehab, and dribble the basketball up and down the court, thoughts of Jason torment me. His smile creeps into my mind with memories of Mark. While goofing around with his friends in college,

Jason's smile had been so broad it crinkled the outside corners of his eyes. With me, his smile, though soft and gentle, ignited a warmth that shone through his hazel brown eyes, a contrast to his powerful 6'2' build and everything one presumes about a football player. I had met Jason at Eastern where he was a defensive back on the football team. Since we were both athletes, we ran into one another frequently in the corridors of Hec-Ed Pavilion. And when we were lucky, or unlucky depending on how you looked at it, we sat next to one another in the training room taping or icing down injuries. I was shy by nature, and with Jason it was no exception. But after seeing one another often, through three years of college together, we had become friends.

I had often wished for more than a friendship. In fact, there was a time when I held Jason close, a stolen hug on a red Honda Enduro, when I thought our relationship might change. We had begun the evening hanging out with friends and the evening ended with my arms encompassing Jason's chiseled waist as he took me for a ride on his motorcycle. The night, dark at first, had opened into an expanse of bright stars and as his Enduro quickly climbed the gentle hill, I clung to him, my chest tight against his back. I felt warm and safe. When we reached the top of the hill and stopped, I ached to have him pull my hands to his lips. I wanted to forget my boyfriend, forget what was right. But all too soon Jason started the bike again and we rode down the gentle hill, returning to our separate lives. Our lives would cross paths, a glance at practice, quick "hellos" on campus or a dance at Showies. And once a lazy walk to my apartment after a campus party full of wanting. But Jason had a girlfriend and I a boyfriend, so our innocent friendship remained just that.

I'm uneasy. I want to see Jason, to talk to him. I know I

shouldn't, but I look in the phone book for his number anyway. It's not there. I call information. There's no Jason Elliott. There's no number for Beecham, the company he'd worked for. I give up, but I still think about him and I'm angry at myself because of it. I should only be thinking of Mark.

Walking the aisle at Costco, I see a bundled three-pack of Aquafresh toothpaste and stop in my tracks. Beecham, Beecham makes AquaFresh toothpaste. I pick up the bundle and scan the packaging. Beecham's now SmithKlineBeecham. I commit the 1-800 number to memory. When I return home I pick up the phone. After being transferred to numerous departments, I find that Jason still works for the company, and before I know it, I'm transferred to his voicemail. I doubt I can work my way through the company maze back to his line, so in a panic I leave a message.

"Hi, this is Sonya," I say, dragging my left index and middle finger across my forehead.

"Gaubinger," I add.

He'd remember a name like Gaubinger, wouldn't he?

"You know, from Eastern."

With my elbow now resting on my kitchen table, I drop my head into the palm of my hand. Closing my eyes, I continue, "I was just thinking about you and thought I'd give you a call."

I search my mind for something reasonable to say. I fail.

"Give me a call sometime. My number is 555-1017."

I have one last chance for something clever. "Bye."

I hold my thumb to the off button and rest the phone gently against my forehead. I have the same sinking feeling I get in the pit of my stomach when I throw a full-court pass and just as I release the pass I realize it's going to be too long. I can't get the pass back and the player won't reach it. I want the pass back. I want my words back. I want to take back everything and continue living my pathetic life.

I wish I hadn't called, yet at the same time I hold an excited energy that is burning to escape.

"I can't feel this way." I scold myself. Sadness and grief are the only emotions I'm allowed; anything other than that is unfair to Mark. Still, I wait and hope.

"Sonya?"

"Yes."

"Hi, this is Jason. Jason Elliott."

My chest tightens as I pull a chair out from the kitchen table and sit down.

"Hi." I say, taking a slow breath before I continue. "I'm glad you called."

"I was really surprised to get your message," Jason says.

"Yeah," I answer, wondering why I got myself into this mess. What was I thinking?

"It was on my internal voicemail. How'd you get that number?"

I tell the story of the long search through the SmithKline-Beecham labyrinth, I don't tell him yet about the baseball game and the catcher.

"I heard you were in an accident," Jason says.

"Yep," I say, running my finger back and forth across my lip.

"I'm sorry," there's a slight hesitation, "about your fiancé."

"Thank you." I say, looking at the small picture of Mark in his Rainer Jersey, on the kitchen counter. I tell Jason about the accident and a little about Mark.

"I thought you were hurt really bad too," he says, opening the conversation to a long dissertation of my injuries which I rattle off with ease.

"Wow," he says. "How's your face look?"

175

"How's my face look?" I return with a giggle.

"I didn't mean..." Jason starts before I interrupt him.

"About the same," I say, knowing he didn't mean anything by the question. "Just a couple scars. But I have big scars from surgery on my arm and leg and an ugly scar on my lower back and butt; they think it's from when I was thrown out the window."

"I can't believe you survived," he says, "and that you're back in Seattle already?"

"I know," I say. Neither can I.

Jason's calls become a welcome part of my daily routine. We laugh about his "how does your face look?" question. Our conversations are easy, like those with a life-long friend. I'm not ready to date and there's no mention of it. It's only after several weeks of chatting on the phone that we decide to meet for lunch.

I haven't had a facial in years and I made the stupid decision to schedule one right before my lunch with Jason. My face has red spots and I'm wearing old shorts and a t-shirt when I pull my car in to my Bellevue Manor parking space, late. On my way to the front door I glance at a Toyota Camry parked against the curb and I'm surprised to have a bright smile peering back at me from beyond the open passenger side window.

"Jason?" I ask, walking toward the car.

Jason hops out. He's dressed in his work clothes. Black slacks, crisp white shirt, and a mahogany tie. He looks stunning. My stomach turns. Then I remember the red spots and my outfit and my shoulders slump a little.

"Wow, you look just like you did in college," he says.

I look down slightly and smile. He's not close enough to see the spots.

"With your shorts and your hair pulled back, you look like

you just came from basketball practice."

My cheeks grow warm. Was that a compliment? From his soft eyes and his genuine smile I can see that it is. After a run-in with a Burlington Northern train engine, I certainly could have looked worse and I'm sure he expected as much.

Lunch is safe ground. Not a "date," not really, and no lengthy time obligation. I have physical therapy scheduled at 2:00 p.m. to keep it that way. Barely touching our food, we talk our way through the meal. The decision to meet for a short lunch seemed like a good one but now that it's time to go I want to spend more time together. Normally, I thrive on my independence but, even if I don't know it, I crave a close friend now more than ever, one who can share in my pain and help in my recovery.

"It was really great to see you," I say, sitting in the passenger seat of his car in front of my physical-therapy office.

"It was great to see you, too," He says.

His pager buzzes.

As Jason peeks at the number on his pager, I admire his face. His straight Roman nose matches his strong jaw. He looks young, vibrant, alive. I feel old, like I've lived a thousand lifetimes. I get out of the car, and with the smell of him lingering by my side, I fear that I might never see him again.

"Thanks for the ride," I call as I step back from the car and wave.

"No problem," Jason says, with a wink and a wave of his hand.

"Talk to you soon," I say, my chest tightening as I watch him drive away.

During physical therapy and on my slow walk home, my heart and mind work over time. Jason won't want to see me again. Talk about carrying baggage. I'm dragging around a trunk weighted with bricks, maybe even tied to a rope that's looped around my neck. He seemed to enjoy himself, but we were reminiscing about old times - he was being polite. Besides, I'm only ready to be friends, nothing more, and most single guys are not okay with "just being friends."

I don't tell a soul I've met a man for lunch. The guilt is unbearable. I reassure myself it doesn't matter, Jason won't call. He calls. Secretly, I'm pleased.

Jason works all day as a sale representative for SmithKline Beecham and keeps busy, much to his dismay, setting toothpaste and mouthwash displays between sales calls. About the time he finishes work each day is the time I leave to massage school. I'm gone from 5:00 p.m. until 11:00 most week nights. (And all day two weekends a month.) A call before massage class is a treat, but usually I have to wait until I return to my apartment late at night. I look forward to Jason's calls. And when he asks me to dinner, I look forward to seeing him again.

Though I had agreed to dinner, as I sit curled up on my love seat looking at the picture of Mark and me holding one another with arms wrapped around our bodies like the bendy rubber toys I had as a kid, arms and legs twisted together, faces stuck in goofy childish grins, I feel sick to my stomach. I can't go on a dinner date. I'm not ready. I won't be comfortable in public. It's too soon. I pick up the delicately carved wood frame, touch the glass to my lips and close my eyes.

All week I'm uneasy. Days pass like the ticking of a bomb. My heart is being torn apart. I think about Jason and what it would be like to have him touch me. To have my starved body take pleasure in his every touch as he discovers each hidden scar. I feel incredible guilt for wanting the physical closeness I miss so much with Mark gone. I'm overwhelmed and decide to cancel our date.

When Jason calls I'm ready to break the news, but he beats me to the punch.

"I was thinking," he begins.

I lean back in my chair and ready myself for the blow. Of what kind, I'm not sure but I've learned to expect the unexpected.

"How about we have dinner at my place? It'll be more comfortable for you, and I'll barbecue or something."

My shoulders relax and I close my eyes.

"That sounds perfect."

I pull into Arbor Crest, an '80s housing development where, just as the trees and foliage are beginning to fill in, the houses have begun to fade and lose their luster. My heart's pounding. I think of Mark, and wonder why I'm here. Wonder how I can show such disrespect. Or would Mark want me to be here? Want me to search for happiness? Jason's house is a light beige house at the far end of a cul-de-sac, and makes a monochromatic statement set beside the varying shades of beige houses that line the wide streets. When I pull into the driveway, the pounding of my heart quickens. Jason greets me as I come to the front door, and leads me in with a touch of his hand. As I look around the three-bedroom house, which he purchased with his best friend (who is conveniently absent), I smile to myself, holding back the urge to comment that now I felt like I'm back in college. His house is pure bachelor décor. Movie posters are stapled near the line of the ceiling, there's a collage of mismatched furniture and a recently acquired Coors Light sign that makes the final statement. On a late night accompanied by a few beers during my college years I would have definitely felt at home but tonight it might have been uninviting had it not been for the tall, handsome man standing next to me.

Mark and I were nearly eye to eye. Jason's tall frame towers over me. When I look up at him and ask to see the rest of the

179

house, I feel safe. I've lost almost an inch of height with the impact of the accident and my muscles still hang on my bones in a way that seems unnatural to me, and though I'm getting stronger physically, my arm is still tender to the touch. Would it hurt to have Jason's arms around me? I want him to try. I want him to gently reach his arms around me, rest his chin along my head, and whisper that everything will be all right. Instead he brings me on a tour of the rest of the house. And for now, just having him near me is enough.

It's nice to relax and enjoy Jason's company. He barbeques three different types of steaks, just for fun, makes a salad of iceberg lettuce, tomatoes and the choice of a bottle ranch or vinaigrette dressing and hot buttered French bread straight from a foil bag. Not a gourmet feast by any means, but just what I need. He serves the dinner on white Corian plates and gives me the full plate with the biggest steak. What he doesn't know is that I was raised on red meat and love it. And that I grew up with a big brother with whom I had to keep up if I wanted much food at meal times. I down my steak before he makes it halfway through his and carry on a conversation at the same time. I explain that when my body is healed I plan to travel to Europe. Listening politely, Jason glances at my plate and then offers me the last steak. I take it.

"How'd you like the steaks?" he asks.

It's not until I look up from my last bite that I realize that he's giving me a hard time.

"Not bad," I say, cowering a little in my seat as I give a peace offering. "You want my last bite?"

"No, thanks," he says, a twinkle in his eyes. "Next time I'll know better than to give you the biggest steak, and then another, before I'm full."

"Sorry," I say. I can almost hear his stomach growling.

Jason reaches his hand across the table and touches mine.

"Really, I don't care," he says before he pulls his hand away. My heart races.

I'm surprised by my desire to kiss Jason when we make our way down the stairs of the split level entry at the end of the night. Almost to the front door, we sit on the carpeted steps and continue our conversation eye to eye. We talk about Jason's job, we talk about my job, we talk for a long time. Then following a lengthy pause Jason takes hold of both my hands and asks if he can kiss me. I nod yes. He moves his hand tenderly over my shoulder, across my back, and into my long blonde hair. Our eyes mingle for a brief moment before he leans forward and presses his lips gently against mine. He looks deep into my eyes, searching for my true answer. I'm still, but inside my body burns with desire.

As his hand pulls gently on my hair, I arch my back and lean into his kiss. My body tingles and I reach my left arm around his waist. His body is muscular and strong, but his kiss is tender, careful. I can tell he's being cautious and it makes me want him more. It makes me wish I could forget the feelings I have lurking in the depth of my soul. Jason feels good, but I'm not allowed to enjoy life now that Mark can't. I try to hold back the tears, but while I'm kissing Jason, tears escape, uncontrolled. I want to leave. I feel like a fool. Jason puts both his arms around me and holds me tight. I cry for everything that has been lost in my life. And most of all I cry for Mark, I miss him desperately. How can I think of opening my heart to Jason, or to anyone for that matter, when there is a pit of sorrow deep in my soul? I cry until evening turns to dawn. All the while Jason runs his hand slowly across my back, somehow absorbing some of my pain until my heart and mind grows clear. And as May's early sunlight begins to shine through the front window pane, I know it's time for me to go. I'm tired, embarrassed, and ridden with guilt, but somehow, with no tears remaining, I'm also filled with hope. Hope of sharing my life with someone, something I haven't felt or wanted since Mark died.

EASY SPIRIT

"I swore I would never do this, it's so humiliating to women," I explain to the woman at the commercial casting agency in charge of the casting for Easy Spirit shoes. Earlier in the week, Lynn had called me from my agency to tell me to wear a short skirt and pumps to a casting for an Easy Spirit commercial. I had told her how stupid I thought their old commercial was, and that I was glad to see that they had decided to change their advertising campaign. While in college, I had watched the Easy Spirit commercial and laughed at the women in goofy pastel outfits, who had obviously never played much basketball, bounce around the court. As a college athlete, I felt the commercial showed women in a bad light. Yes, it was the 80's, but woman athletes were making huge strides and being taken seriously and I felt the commercial had been a definite step backward.

Twenty models, all dressed to kill, had waited anxiously in the sparse room. I had tugged at my tight skirt and stared at the movie posters on the wall, until I was called into the back room. Now standing in tall black pumps, a tight black skirt with a body hugging shirt I state my name and agency and then roll my eyes and laugh out loud at the next request.

"Yes, I can dribble a basketball."

I'm square to the camera, calves bulging in my pumps, when the casting agent tosses me a ball. I catch it with a familiarity that drives away the usual anxiety I feel during a casting. I dribble the ball between my legs and behind my back. My arm moves with much less pain now, as long as I keep it low and near my body. And in short order I demonstrate to the casting agent quite positively, that yes, I can dribble a basketball.

I leave the casting agency, climb into my Scirocco and sit thinking of what this commercial could mean to me. "They've got to pick me for this thing," I say to myself as I put my car into gear. It's the first time in my career that I've allowed myself to worry over a casting after leaving. It's normal for me to be nervous before a casting, but once I walk out the door, I let it go. Today's different. I need this job. Money's tight. I've been on my own for four months and I'm trying to get by with all the regular bills, health club membership, and an onslaught of medical bills that are nearing $50,000 as well as my new massage school tuition. It doesn't matter that I can't move my right arm up to shoulder height, my shooting arm, I know basketball. I'm perfect for the job!

After two call-back auditions to the casting agency and no news, I'm beside myself. I get a page from my agency as I'm driving into Bellevue for a Nordstrom informal modeling job. I spy a phone booth across the street and flip a U-turn into the Chevron station. My heart's pounding as I dig frantically through the ashtray for a quarter and then run to the phone booth.

"They booked you for the Easy Spirit commercial," Lynn says as soon as I'm on the line. She knows how much I need this commercial. It's a national commercial spot and if everything goes well, if the commercial actually runs, it could be very lucrative. It could easily pay all my medical bills, and then some.

"Thanks," I say with an audible sigh, "I'll call you back for the details after my job."

I hang up the phone and for a moment the weight of the world has been lifted from my shoulders. As I walk back to my car, as hard as I try not too, I begin to cry.

The commercial's shot on location at an old grade-school gym in Ballard the following week. Rays of broken light spread across the tattered hardwood and I feel like I'm on the set of Hoosiers. The woman who's supposed to guard me sprains her ankle warming up in her high heel pumps and all the other players' toes are beginning to blister. The production company chooses another player from the extras and we match up and amble onto the court in our pumps to film the commercial. Some of the takes seem unrealistic to me, but I'm hesitant to step on anyone's toes. Then as usual, I can't keep my mouth shut, and I take measures to make sure my bad arm doesn't come into play during filming.

"We could run a give and go here," I point to where I would need to catch the return pass, "and then I could cross over for a left-handed hook."

The director decides to give it a try on the next take. Now, wearing pumps, I shoot with my off hand at a hoop with no backboard. In the place of the backboard is an incredibly expensive wide angle lens held in check by the photographer's face. We film several takes and I make nearly every shot. It's a wrap. Easy Spirit is happy and we all limp off the court in pain.

Shooting the Easy Spirit commercial had been fun, which is not always the case with modeling. Modeling often has more downs than ups. Castings for jobs can be brutal. It's degrading to have someone briskly page through your portfolio, yawn briefly, and hand it back to you without looking you in the eye or gaping in horror when a size 6 dress fits tight around the middle. The jobs themselves depend mostly upon the crew. Is the crew excited about a shoot? Is there a positive atmosphere back stage? Is there stability and focus on set or are there too many chiefs all putting in their two bits, all questioning the direction of the models and the photographers who then all begin to question themselves? Why did I choose such a crazy career? I feel comfortable in front of the camera and on the runway but modeling, of course, is all about your looks and I don't like being judged by my looks. In fact, because of this, I rarely tell people I'm a model. Modeling is my job, the way I make money. Modeling is flexible, it can be a lot of fun and the pay is excellent (when I work,) and occasionally it's an ego booster, like having an awesome basketball game. It's just a small part of who I am, but an important part since everything in my life has been lost. Getting back into the world of modeling has become a part of my healing. Filming the national Easy Spirit commercial, a commercial that will likely eliminate my financial worries and bring new stability to my life, is a miracle.

※

I drive past Jason's exit. The song Forever Young is blaring on the radio. May the good lord be with you down every road you roam. The words from Mark's memorial tape sting. An aching begins in my lower jaw and moves into my throat. It settles deep in my chest and burns. My eyes well with tears. Salty trails run down my face and fall to my chest.

I take the next exit and pull into the darkest corner of a 7- Eleven parking lot. The music has changed but I can't hear it anymore. I drop my forehead onto the bony knuckles of my hands that are clammy against the steering wheel. I search my mind for a vivid picture of Mark but it eludes me. I want to see him as if he were there standing in front of me, but I can't. I can see only one part of him, his calves. Strong, defined. I see them on the basketball court. I see them bounding up the stairs in front of me. I can almost feel them. But I can't see his face. Not like I used to and it kills me inside.

I reach to the locket that hangs down from my neck. Mark's youngest sister gave it to me, and as much as I love it, I hate that I have to open it. But I have to, now. I pry open the silver locket and try to memorize every tiny detail, again. How can his beautiful face escape me?

Sobs turn to occasional gasps for air and through swollen eyes I look at the clock on my dash board. 5:30, I'm not late yet. I gather myself and dry my tears. I have time, Jason's just now expecting me and it's a long drive from the Seattle to Woodinville in traffic, so it's not unusual to run late. I close the locket and my eyes and wait. Before long I turn the Scirocco around and head back down the freeway to Jason's exit.

When I pull up, Jason's sitting on the front porch with a beer in his hand and another on the rail.

"It's cold," he says, pointing to the beer. But instead of bringing mine to me he sets his down and walks over and gives me a hug. I feel a twinge in my shoulder with his gentle squeeze, but I want his arms around me.

"How was the drive?" he asks, taking a closer look at my face.

"Lots of traffic,"

"You okay?"

"Yeah, I'm alright," I say, before stepping back and walking over to sit on the front porch.

"Bad news with your attorney?" Jason asks, pulling up beside me.

"No, not really."

"School okay?"

"I have class all next weekend which sucks, but yes, it's fine." I reach for the beer and have a drink. "I'm just having a tough day."

Jason kisses me on the forehead, "I'm sorry, Sōn."

Sōn. I rest my head against his chest and cry.

187

I recognize my parents' van as we pull into the parking lot. Jason and I are meeting them at a hotel in Bellevue before continuing, as a group, to Yakima for a little wine tasting tour. A little wine tasting might be an understatement, because after all, it is my 26th birthday, and the Gaubinger's enjoy a good drop of wine. It's the perfect opportunity for Jason to get to know my family and them Jason. Gathered in the hotel room, Jason pulls out a neatly wrapped box, a bit larger than a shoe box, and hands it my way.

"I thought we should start your birthday early," he says.

I'm not sure he's making a good impression, we aren't celebrating yet. But I thank him and open the package anyway and find a brand new Sony video camera.

"Wow," is all I can muster at first. "It's such a nice gift. It's too nice."

"I got a really good deal on it through Tami-Su's husband: plus," he pauses, "it comes with a cruise to Jamaica."

"Right."

"No really, we get a great discount on a cruise," he says, all eyes upon him.

"I don't know, Jason," I love the gift but it feels like too much. "I don't know if I can accept such an expensive gift."

"Well," he looks at me and only me with a sparkle in his eyes. "The gift, all of it, is for me too."

All I can say is thank you and I'm glad because I do love the gift. I love the video camera but more so, I love the idea of getting away from Seattle and my life, with Jason by my side.

Jason fits in with my parents. I'm surprised at how easily he chats and jokes with them both. My mom has met him once, and sees that he has brought me some joy. I know my dad will be cautious allowing another man into my life, but he too understands that Jason is good for me.

After tasting and toasting wines in celebration of my life and the 26 years I have been in it, we return to our normal lives. Jason and I grow closer everyday. I have massage school until 11:00 p.m. most nights, but we talk on the phone when I get home, or drive to one another's places to be together. I love for Jason to kiss me and hold me. I love to spoon with him through the night, to be together when we awaken. But I'm not ready to make love and Jason understands. Jason knows almost everything about me now. I say almost, because there is much about my heart and soul that I can never explain. The pain of loss. The ache deep inside for a life that will never be. With my recent financial stability at work and Jason by my side, my spirit is more at ease, but I'm afraid there will always be a part of me that is missing.

LOVE IS NOT LIKE PIE

Looking at the pile of unpaid medical bills, notices to vacate, and my massage notebook that I haven't opened all week, I wonder how I will manage. How can a 26-year-old broken-down widow do it all? That's what I feel like, not all the time these days, but much of the time. I reach for my massage book then push it away and walk to my room, crawl into bed, pull the covers over my head and cry. It isn't until the last huffing breath leaves my mouth that I lift the covers and open my eyes. Reaching to my bedside table, I pick up the new black journal with the brass binding, given to me by my friend Moon and decide to dirty the journal's pages. I sit up in bed, squeeze a pillow behind me and begin to write.

October 20th, 1992

One year ago Mark was killed. God, I miss him.
I've worked so hard to get my life back on track, but
it will never be the same. There will always be sadness
in my heart. It's been a long time since I've written
and I can tell. I need to write. I've worked so hard
to get better. I have a great family, great friends and
Jason, oh what I would do without him I don't know,

but there is still an emptiness that feels like it will be there forever.

I miss you, Mark. I feel so alone.

I put the journal back where I found it. Then scoot down into the covers and roll onto my good side. I know it's going to be a long day.

Crawling out of bed, I stare at the clock and wonder. Not how I have managed to stay in bed until 10:30 but how I got this far. How could a year have gone by? How could all this time have passed without Mark? Time stopped with Mark's death, at first anyway, and now I am here, living my life and he is not.

How can I be certain his memory won't slip away forever? It's already hard to see his face clearly without a picture, at times. I struggle to remember what it felt like, smelled like, to have him lying next to me, holding me. I hate to admit it even to myself, but it's true. If I can't bring Mark back, I need to bring his memory to life. I need to do something, something in his memory.

His family and friends started the Mark Overholt Memorial Scholarship Fund which grants a scholarship to a student/athlete from Mark's high school. But I'm not a part of it. I feel like an outsider, awkward. But I'm not sure I have the energy to do something on my own. I decide to write a letter to my family and friends asking for money to support the fund. It feels wrong, but it's something, so I begin to write. Or at least I try until the phone rings. I let out a sigh of relief.

"Hi, J." I say, as soon as I hear his voice.

"How are you doing?" Jason asks, knowing today will be tough but also knowing I want my space.

"All right." I fib. "I have so much to do around here. It's keeping my mind occupied."

"How'd the models meeting go last night?" he asks, knowing the work I have put into organizing it and hoping it hasn't added to the stress of today. The models meeting had been organized by Kelle and me, after numerous conversations with different groups of runway models who were concerned about Seattle's low rates. The rates hadn't changed in 20 years and many of us hoped it might be a possible to make a change. Kelle and I had decided it couldn't hurt to have a gathering of models from different agencies and discuss the problem. I had put together a handout on the breakdown of our rates and what in the end was our take-away pay to present at the meeting and we had good showing from all the different modeling agencies in town.

"Oh, the meeting went pretty good."

"What did you guys decide to do?"

"Well, there were a couple of good ideas. We could have our agents take a stand on our behalf, have them write a letter to the big dogs threatening a walk-out for runway shows or all the models could turn down the booking for the next big show. It would have to include everyone and I just don't know if everyone would really do it. Models from all the agencies came and everyone agreed that we should do something, but we'll see what happens. I'm just afraid Kelle and I will take the brunt of this thing if something goes wrong."

"What do you mean? It doesn't sound like you even made any decisions."

"Oh, I know. I just wonder why I even got involved. I really don't care that much, I'm just sick of the complaining. I mean, I agree that by the time we pay our agent, parking, and taxes we end up with half our rate. We don't work everyday, we don't have insurance and..." I walk to the couch and plop down. "Let's talk about something else."

"How'd your shoot go, the one on the sailboat," Jason asks.

I look across the room at my favorite picture of Mark. He's smiling at me, daring me to smile back. Wanting me to be happy.

"Oh, it was good," I say, pulling my soft knit throw across my legs, "but it was freezing!"

The shoot had lasted most of the windy October day, on a sailboat that raced across the cold waters of the Puget Sound. All of us models wore vacation cruise wear, but our red noses and goose bumps seemed to me would have been evidence that we were not on vacation.

"My arm and leg were killing me. I'm not one to complain on a shoot, but I could barely handle it. The longer I was out there the more my body ached. I sat in a hot bath for an hour when I got home, just to get warm enough to go to the models meeting," I shiver again just thinking about it. "Sorry I didn't call when I got home last night, I was exhausted."

I didn't feel the need to tell Jason I watched the videotape of Mark's funeral again. That I had spent the night and all morning dreading the idea of living. Not that I wanted to take my life, I just didn't want to partake in the living of it, at least not today. That was how I felt until just this moment, the moment I talked to Jason.

I'm unaware of the tall pines that line the highway as I near Everett. I feel guilty for not returning sooner. And when I pull up to the curb and look across to Mark's grave that's covered with flowers, a spear is driven through my heart. I'm a bad mourner. Where is my dedication? It must look like I never loved Mark, that I don't love him. But I do. I do love him. I will love him for the rest of my life. I stand under the silent gray sky; the cool wind caressing my back as I shake, working to hold back tears. I walk with an even step to Mark's grave site. The grave is a flurry of color; I bend to add a dozen Sonia roses to my liking amongst the rest. My right leg aches. In the silence I wonder how it is that I have always been alone in the cemetery when I come alone, but I am thankful.

"God, Mark, I miss you," I whisper before tears escape, turning whispers to sobs. I lower to my knees and stay for a long time. I think about Mark and about his family. Mark's family knows that I am dating someone. They don't know who, they haven't met him, but they know. What do they think about it? About me? Once, when Larry and Joan had first visited me in Spokane after the accident, Larry had sat next to my hospital bed in my parent's living room and said, "You must go on with your life, Sonya. Someday you will find someone you love to share your life with. Mark would want that." I hadn't believed him. I hadn't wanted to go on with my life. It had been too soon to hear such a notion. But now that I was trying to go on with my life, would Larry, and Joan, agree? I couldn't talk to them about it. I could barely comprehend it all myself.

Arriving at the front doorstep of the Overholts a bit late, I wipe the corners of my eyes. Larry opens the door with a warm smile then wraps his arms around me.

It's a long time before he lets go.

"Glad you could come," he says.

"I wouldn't miss it," I reply just as he lets go and leads me up the stairs.

"Come on up," he says. "Chris is here, and so is Mickey."

I follow him up the split level stairs that leads from the entry to the kitchen and living room. The same set of stairs I had watched Mark's firm calves ascend each time we came to visit his parents. I push the memory away. I can't go there right now.

Mark's friends and family are all gathered around the kitchen table. It's comfortable and warm, but something is missing. Mark of course, but something else. A heavy weight is pushing me down.

"Excuse me," I whisper, into the conversation, while I back my chair from the table and move silently to the bathroom. Once in, door locked, I lean forward, grip both hands on the edge of the sink, drop my head and begin to cry. The more I try to stop, the harder and faster the tears come. Until there are no more. I wipe my face and wait. I wait for the pain in my heart to subside, return then subside. I excuse myself from the table two more times before hugging Mark's family and friend's goodbye. During the long drive to Jason's I find I'm continually gasping for air and it's only after I'm tight in his arms that I'm alright.

❋

Physical therapy is a bore, but at least in combination with workouts at the gym, I'm seeing results. My arm is gaining mobility and I'm walking smoothly, with less pain. But I'm a wreck. From the outside things look good, I'm a model after all. But on the inside there is a war going on.

I want Jason to understand me emotionally, even if I don't, so I ask him to see a counselor with me. It isn't the first time I've seen a counselor since the accident, but now that I'm in a relationship, it is the first time I really felt like I need one. I thought I was doing well, thought I was ready to give my heart and soul to Jason. But each time we try to make love, it ends in disappointment. I feel like I'm cheating on Mark. I can't live my life this way, nor can I ask Jason to. Crying is normal in my circumstance, but going on with my life? Now that is a different story.

Willingly by my side, Jason escorts me to the counselor's office. The first visit seems short, almost awkward—a quick overview and introduction: but waiting for our second visit, in the compact waiting room, with no view of the outside world, we hold hands and sit relaxed against our seats. Even though I'm not sure it will make a difference, I'm thankful Jason is here. Things are good with Jason and me, but I want them to be better, and since I don't know if I'm ready, really ready, to give myself to our relationship, I want help to find out.

"I don't know about this," Jason says, his eyes squinting and his lips in an exaggerated frown, "I don't think I can listen to Dr. Z with that hair."

"Jason," I hush him, rolling my eyes.

"I mean it; she looks like Kramer from Seinfeld. I can't stop watching her hair bounce around up there when she's talking," he says. "I really don't think we even need to be here."

"Bear with me, I need to be here," I say. "And since I want 'us' to be good, better than good, we need to be here."

"Okay," he says as the door opens and a young couple, studying the tan carpet on their way out, walk through the waiting room.

Jason and I enter the office and sit across the desk from Dr. Z. Jason is right, we could have been on the set of Seinfeld with Kramer's sister. But before long, I have forgotten about her hair and focus on Jason and me. I need to let go of my past: not let go, I suppose, but be willing to go on. Realize that I have to move forward. But how can I explain to Jason that I just get sad sometimes. That the pain will grab me when I'm driving by a baseball diamond, wearing a wedding dress for a runway show, hearing a train whistle under the viaduct, inhaling fragrance from the Nordstrom men's cologne counter on my way to a fitting, or for no reason at all. Sometimes it's just the fact that it has been too long since I've last cried. How can Jason understand? Why should he? How can he go on living like this?

"How are you feeling, Jason?" asks Dr. Z.

"Good," he answers.

She waits.

"What do you mean?" he asks.

"How do you feel when Sonya thinks about Mark or cries about Mark?" she pushes.

"I understand. It can't be easy for her."

"But what about you? Does it bother you that she thinks about Mark?" she continues.

"No, but it just seems like it should be getting better, or easier for her," Jason answers.

"Let me give you an example that I think might be helpful," she begins, leaning forward on the desk before lifting her hands to form a circle. "Imagine a pie."

I imagine Jason's mind whirling, Kramer with an imaginary pie in her face.

"Love is not like a pie." She waits, looking him in the eye, then glancing towards me, "Sonya doesn't have one big piece of love for Mark, a bunch for her family, and a tiny little slice of love left for you."

She stops, tilts her head a bit, and raises her thick eyebrows.

"The more you love, the more love you have to give."

Jason is quiet and nods his head in agreement. I'm not certain he agrees, but I think it brilliant. The more you love, the more love you have to give. I rest my hand on Jason's. He turns to me and gives me a gentle kiss.

PERFECT

Driving across I-520 on my way to my 6:00 a.m. Nike show at Bellevue Nordstrom, I can hardly keep my eyes open. Yesterday I had been ratted out as the organizer of a model mutiny to Carol and Helen at Nordstrom, reason enough for a sleepless night but when my head had finally hit the pillow at 1:30 a.m., there had been a knock at the door. It had been Mark's sister Debbie. Seeing her would normally be a pleasant surprise, but I had a 4:30 a.m. wake up call and Jason was asleep in my bedroom. Debbie had gone out in Seattle and hadn't wanted to risk the 30-mile drive north to Everett, so there she was on my doorstep hoping to spend the night. After talking with her for a bit I got her set up on the couch and went to bed. In the morning, while I showered, I pondered on what to do, Jason was in my room and Debbie, who didn't know I was in a relationship, let alone a serious one, was asleep on the couch. In the end I had asked Jason to hang out in my room since it was the weekend, and hoped for the best. I was too tired to think of a better solution. Now pulling into a parking spot, I feel sick to my stomach.

Once back stage, for the Bellevue Nordstrom's Nike show, I find my clothes, drop off my bag, then search for Helen hoping to mend fences, hoping information from the models meeting hasn't warped drastically as it made its way through the grapevine. Of course, it has. I try to explain my side of the story as best I can and return to my rack backstage for the start of the show. After ten changes in very tight outfits, I leave Nordtrom, sure I will never work there again, then return to my apartment to learn that Debbie had found Jason in my bed.

Fortunately I have something to look forward to. Mark's older sisters, Wendy and Vikki will be stopping by the apartment with baby Mark. Baby Mark, Vikki's son who was born the summer after Mark died, is my godson. I don't know if I can fulfill the role of godparent. I'm not Catholic. I don't know what a godparent does. My brother's godfather left him a beautiful Austrian coin. I'm planning to buy baby Mark something special but is that enough? I hope there won't be an end to my role as a godparent. Since I'm not able to bear Mark's namesake, I'll do my best to be a part of his life. And tonight Jason will be here. I'm thankful that Jason will be introduced to Mark's other sisters on better terms.

❄

The sun and a bowl of chilimac, that Jason's whipped up for lunch, warms me as we sit on the deck. The view of Mt. Baker is brilliant. It's late October and I'm reminded of a warm fall day just over a year ago when Mark and I had departed from my parents' home in Spokane. Mark had worn shorts that day. I set my hand on Jason's bare leg and take a deep breath then move my spoon around in my bowl. Jason scoots his chair next to mine and put his arm around me. Lyle Lovett's words penetrate my mind—Here I am, yes it's me; take my hand and you'll see—and break my spell. Nuzzling my cheek into Jason's shoulder, I close my eyes.

"I love you, Jason," I say. And I mean it. I'm still afraid. Still unsure of what I want in the future. Will I ever want to get married? Can I really commit myself to Jason? I'm not sure, but I do know I love him.

"I love you too, Sōn" he says. And before he has to worry about the conversation getting too serious he stands up and takes the dishes into the kitchen. From the kitchen he hollers, "Hey, you want to shoot some hoops?"

"Sure," I answer, wanting to be on the court with Jason, but wishing I could do more than rebound and dribble.

"There's a great hoop down by the slew."

We start to change into our basketball gear, but being young, in love and partially clothed, we become distracted. First Jason pulls me close and gives me a kiss, a hard kiss that sends shivers up my spine. I forget about basketball. I kiss him back, leaning into his strong body. Then I push myself away, heart pounding and sit on the edge of the bed. I find it hard to breathe. I look into Jason's eyes and he knows what I'm thinking. He leans forward, and reaching his arm around my back he moves me on to the bed, and gently rests his body on mine. His heart is beating louder than mine. I give him a gentle smile and another kiss. Though a small part of me is restless and unsure, when we make love I see and feel Jason, and only Jason.

By the time we drive to the slew the sun is low in the sky. Long shadows reach from our bodies and extend nearly the width of the court. I hold the basketball and then turn it slowly in my hands, feeling every bump of leather skim across my finger tips. This moment in time is perfect. Perhaps my senses are heightened because of making love, but I can hear the rustle of the Birch trees down by the slew as if I were climbing in them. I can smell the leather basketball, even with the fresh cut grass on the side of the court. I look at Jason. He's standing at the top of the key, waiting for me to pass him the ball. He is striking. With his wide shoulders and narrow hips he looks taller than 6' 2". He has a strong face that's still darkened from the sun and I'm reminded of why I was so attracted to him when I first saw him in college, when I looked down the corridor of Hec Ed Pavilion and made eye contact with him as he sauntered, head held high, on his way to football practice. As I have gotten to know him better, he has become even more attractive. But there is something to be said about that first look, the first moment you see someone and feel that attraction for them. At this moment I'm reminded of that time.

"I'm open," Jason taunts, clapping his hands for the ball.

I snap a pass into his hands and then jab in his direction before I turn to rebound the ball. Jason takes a few steps then relocates for my next pass. He works his way around the court, and even as the rebounder I'm having fun. I try a shot with my right arm, but it's painful and I don't have enough strength and flexibility to get the ball to the hoop. I shoot a few with my left hand. It's not easy. The fact that I made my shots at the Easy Spirit shoot is a surprise. I can tell that it will be a long while before I can get on a court and play, I mean really play. When Jason and I leave the court I'm hot, happy and hungry for dinner.

We walk back to the car hand in hand. Jason leans against the car and pulls my hips to him before he kisses me on the forehead. I give him a hug then lean back.

"I'm hungry. What should we have for dinner?" I ask.

"How about Mexican?" Jason suggests. "A margarita sure sounds good."

"Sounds good to me too," I answer, and then correct myself, "no, it sounds perfect."

I don't mean just the dinner choice, perfect is how I feel about the entire afternoon.

GAME ON

Twisting my forearm back and forth I look at my shoulder and watch the skin move as if a mole is just beneath the surface. It moves back and forth, back and forth, and with each move there's also a sudden pop. Not too painful, just irritating. The screw that holds the rod in place in my arm, snaps across the tendon. The more mobility I gain in my shoulder, the worse it gets. Dr. Perry had explained that it isn't necessary that I remove the screw, but because I'm active, it might be a good idea. The tendon will become increasingly irritated with the constant rubbing across the pin. "You can remove it in a year," he had said. That year has passed.

I kiss Jason goodbye. As I'm rolled into the operating room in Deaconess Hospital, Spokane, a chill sweeps through my body. The joking around in the waiting room is over. Now it's just me. I'm back in the hospital, on my own accord, and I don't like it. By the time my right arm is prepped and numbed and a screen is in place to keep my arm from view, my mouth is dry. When Dr. Perry drags the scalpel across my skin my heart is pounding. But it's only when I feel the intense pressure of the instrument, that must look like a screwdriver, unscrewing the pin from the rod (and bone) that I question my insistence on using local anesthesia. Because of this decision, however, I'm out of the hospital and shopping for underwear (which I'd forgotten to pack) in less than an hour.

Because I feel good the day after surgery, we decide to make the drive to the Tri-Cities to Jason's sister's house for a Halloween party. We borrow a couple of my mom and dad's costumes. They have a closet full of costumes to choose from because they attended Fasching (a German costume ball) every year. Jason chooses a Court Jester outfit and I settle on the Broadway musical cat. Jason puts on black tights and a black and white knee-length costume with bells on the pointed hem and matching pointed shoes with bells on the toes. Mom and I paint his face black and white with diamonds of opposing colors around his eyes, and then finish off the look with a black-and-white hat with three long curved points, each ringing with bells. I'm wearing a tight black body suit from neck to toe that's accented by tufts of fur at my wrists and ankles, a long braided tail, a black wig with ears, and carefully detailed black and white face paint that transforms me into a five-foot-nine alley cat.

Mom and Dad take pictures, kiss us good-bye and send us on our way. Two hours later we pull into Tri-cities and are cracking our first beers surrounded by ghosts and goblins, all strangers to me. Introductions are easy, dressed as a cat. Perched near Jason's side, I simply outstretch a paw and draw my whiskers into a smile. As the evening progresses, however, the party changes. It becomes louder and louder as the alcohol flows, and the louder the party becomes the more I need to curl up into a quiet corner.

Jason is across the room when his sister, Michele, dressed in a Toga, reaches across my back. I lean forward afraid she might accidentally hit my arm. A red devil stands across from us, her beer nearly empty.

"This is Jason's girlfriend, Sonya," Michele says to the devil. I reach out my left hand and shake her hand as best I can. "Hi," I say.

"Sonya's a model," Michele adds and I cringe, knowing I'm now assumed, at the very best, to be stupid.

I don't say anything.

"Oh," is the little devil's response, with an accompanying sneer as she glances at my slender body that hasn't gained back its usual strength and size since the accident. "That explains it."

"That explains what, you bitch?" I say to myself.

My life is not model perfect. Only yesterday morning I had the second surgery from an accident where I lost my fiancé and almost lost my life.

I smile and listen to more boisterous chatter for a few minutes and then excuse myself and slip out the front door. The cool air feels good against my chest. It even helps hold back the tears until I reach the end of the driveway where I stay until my fingers grow numb. By the time I return to the party Jason is in full swing, energized by the people and the beer and excited to have me back by his side. I only wish he could see my eyes screaming, "Get me out of here!"

I'm happy to be home at Bellevue Manor, even though the tenant who pulled a knife on Jason and me a month earlier has left me an obscene phone message. At least I have my own space. The Halloween party was too much, too soon. I'm looking forward to being home alone for a day, and then tomorrow meeting my dad for our Tuesday lunch. After that I'll try to catch up on school and the apartment complex before I go to Vashon Island to spend the weekend with Grandma and Grandpa Lowry.

At Grandma and Grandpa's I play bingo, of course, but without Mark by my side, I have very little luck. But I do have fun. We relax in the cabin. We attend church. My thoughts linger on Mark and the upcoming anniversary of what was supposed to be our wedding day. By the time I leave for Seattle, I feel closer to Grandma and Grandpa Lowry, and in a way, to Mark. But as I board the ferry, I can't stop thinking about Grandpa. He looks frail and I can see that some life has drained from his aging body since Mark died. With grandpa's history of cancer, Mark would have been worried too.

November 8th, 1992

I spent the day by myself; in fact I spent the last four days by myself. I told Jason I needed some time alone. I didn't want to have to cry to him on my wedding day, it didn't seem right. But tonight, Jason stopped by and I did.

I just can't help thinking about what might have been. Mark and I might be expecting our first child and be looking for a house together. We'd have spent our anniversary toasting our good fortune with a bottle of sparkling cider.

Mark, I wish you were here. How I'm supposed to go on without you?

Having the pin removed from my arm has been a good thing. My shoulder moves with less tenderness which makes rehab easier. I'm looking forward to better movement, and perhaps one day a better jump shot. Having the pin out makes it less painful when I'm giving massages, which is beneficial since I have to give at least two a week for school. I gave Jason and Rob, his roommate, a massage last week and my arm felt great. But when Jason and I went to a football game in Zillah, where it seemed like 30 below, my arm had ached with pain.

Every part of my body had hurt. I realize that my injuries will always haunt me. I will never move anywhere cold, but I do want to move. I'm sick of Bellevue Manor.

I'm sick of Bellevue Manor, I'm sick of work, I'm sick of school, I'm sick of rehab, and now I'm even sick of Jason. I slam the door of my apartment on my way to the gym, leaving Jason inside. He can let himself out, and never come back as far as I am concerned. Jason may not understand how I feel about modeling, how as an athlete and college graduate, I feel that my looks are the least of my assets. But he can at least humor me. Especially today, when I'm on the edge. Instead he pokes and prods. "I would tell everyone I met I was a model. I would dress to show off my boobs." I'm certain he would, but Jason is not a woman and he doesn't know how it feels to be treated less than equal. To be treated like you don't have a mind or feelings for that matter. My looks only tell people, in no uncertain terms, that I'm what some might consider "perfect." And I'm not perfect, in fact, I feel like I'm slipping from reality into a nightmare. I want my old life back. I want Mark and the future we had planned together.

I throw open the locker-room door, toss my back pack and car keys in the locker and sit on the long wooden bench reminiscent of my past. Unable to tie my shoe on the floor because of my arm, I set my foot up on the bench and lace my hightops one at a time, tying the locker key into the second shoe. I will do my regular workout then see if I can get in a game. I don't care if I can't shoot, or if it hurts to get bumped, today I'm going to play.

Men gather around the court, tossing up shots and eyeing the competition. I'm thankful there's a sign-up sheet; I'm not in the mood to jockey for a spot on a team. When there are more than ten players on the court a stout man sways over to the sign up sheet and calls off names. Ten names go by and I'm not one of them.

"Excuse me." I say, ball resting on my hip, "You didn't call my name. It's Sonya"

"Oh, I didn't know you wanted to play," he answers, receiving a chuckle from the men closest to him.

"Hence, my name on the list," I reply.

There's more jockeying of the list as men battle to be on the team without the woman, sitting out a game if they have to. How I wish I could shoot the ball with my right arm, but I take what I have, and step on the court. It's like being home. Even from the very start, from the fight to get on the floor, I love it; I love what it does for my body inside and out. I'm now lost, if only for a moment, in the depth of what drives me through life. I can't shoot and have a tough time passing, but playing defense is made easier by the fact that I'm guarding the squat of a man that tried to cut me out of the game. My mind is up for the challenge and fortunately my hip and leg hold up too. By the time I'm finished, the team with "a girl" has won three games. I've taken a few good bumps and I'm sore, but I have been able to play and as I walk off the court giving my teammates left-handed high fives, my heart is rapt in an intensity that captures my spirit and holds at bay the loneliness, the loss, and the past.

I'm in good spirits when I drive to the gym the following Tuesday. Not only because I get to vent my frustrations on the basketball court again, but because Jason remains a part of my life. He had been waiting at my apartment to work things out after our fight. He still thought I should flaunt that I was a model and I didn't, so we agreed to disagree. We also decided to spend Thanksgiving apart, me with my family in Spokane and he with his family in Cashmere. Today as I step on the court and the lunch crowd begins to form, I feel good about the decision, good about spending some time apart, yet I know I will miss him.

Players, mostly businessmen on lunch break, shoot around at both ends of the court. I had gained a couple of friends and at least one enemy playing the other day, but fortunately the stout comedian isn't in sight. A lot of men, perhaps some of the ones warming up right now, believe a woman shouldn't be on the basketball court with men. In fact, it might even ruin their day to have me here. But these men don't understand that life is about doing what you love, which to me means playing basketball, whether I'm playing with men, women, or children. Since Mark died, it's all I have to live for. I try to get on the court as much as possible. I'm not a strong player any more, but I can play, and for that I am happy.

❋

I sob as I pass Tokio exit. The open fields are grey and dark clouds loom overhead. It looks nothing like it did the day Mark and I took this exit just over a year ago. I've driven by the accident site before, but not alone. Not in a situation where I was free to cry. So today I cry. I cry for everything I have lost. There are reasons to be thankful but I can't think of them now. The pain in my heart is unbearable, like when I first learned Mark had died. It makes it nearly impossible to drive, but as I continue down the highway to Spokane the flow of tears lessens and I see once again that I will survive the sorrow and the pain. When I reach my parents' house thirty minutes later, my heart is calm.

Thanksgiving is a time to give thanks. I'm thankful that I have Jason in my life and thankful that my body is healing. I'm thankful to spend time with my family, share stories with Mom and Dad and Putz and Loré. I'm thankful that I have their support, but still as we gather around the dinner table, it doesn't seem right to be giving thanks when so much has been lost.

❋

My skin burns from the heat as I step onto the tarmac. It's

a good burn; as it reaches my bones it takes away the ache that has been following me all winter. A week in Arizona, on Nike, is just what I need. And when I find I will be doing shows for ACG (All Condition Gear) of Nike, which will have fewer runway shows, which means more free time, I know it can't be better.

Walking in front of a big crowd and looking like a jock is easy for me, the only thing that's difficult is making the changes with my bad arm. It still takes a lot of work to maneuver my right shoulder in and out of tight sports tops, but I manage.

The first break I get, I take out on my own to hike Camelback Mountain. When I had last talked to Jason, he had been drinking and by the end of the conversation I wasn't sure where our relationship stood. The conversation had started with I love yous, but as it continued, I learned that Jason didn't believe I loved him. He wondered how long I would be grieving. I didn't know how to answer him. He was my life now, but I couldn't give him an answer that I didn't know. Just when I thought our relationship was on track I realized it was a wreck, a proverbial train wreck.

With a heavy heart I begin the long jog through the neighborhood of red rock and cactus yards to the base of Camelback Mountain. Sweat builds at my temples. When I reach the base of the mountain, the sun has found its way down in the western sky and though it's still hot, I'm relieved to have some shade. I'm also relieved to have had the chance to run things about Jason over in my mind. I stop and inhale deeply, then let the air escape. Let it go, Sonya. The hike is long and I keep an even pace hopping over dry dirt and rocks that seem foreign to me. With each step the tension slips from my body. As I reach the first small plateau, I stop to get a drink and soak in the beauty of the barren land. While staring into the horizon, tears suddenly brake from hiding and come pouring down my cheeks. Memories of Mark have found their way back to the surface of my mind. I find a wide rock, away from the trail, and its travelers, and stand facing the falling sun, until my tears are gone. Gathering myself, I move slowly upward, and then quicken my pace in hopes of a bird's eye view of the sunset.

Once perched on the highest rock I can find, my mind wanders back to Mark. When I think of him now, it's no longer like a Technicolor movie, I mostly see his face from pictures I have in a photo album. Motionless; without the energy and life he carried so strong in his body. It makes me miss him more. How can even his memories slip away; isn't it enough to have lost him? I think there can be no more tears, but they come again until the burnt skies turn a dark red and I have to go.

Hunting for the perfect foothold on the way down becomes a challenge. The shadows are deceiving and my head has begun to swoon. I stop frequently, letting dizzy spells pass. Tightness spreads across my chest when I realize my right hand is beginning to swell. What is going on? Each time I stop I lift my arm above my head in hopes of helping circulation or whatever might be the cause of this new phenomenon. I'm able to finish the hike and make my way back to the hotel. I close the door to my room as the red haze turns dark, but because of my history with sports injuries, quickly go in search of the ice machine. I wrap my shoulder in ice, prop my hand above my head and over time the swelling subsides. I understand now that peculiar pains and aches will always be a part of my life. Setting the ice in the sink, I walk to the edge of the bed and remove my shoes. Now that my hand is better I relax onto the bed. Physical exertion, especially on a basketball court or in nature, has always helped me cope with life. I need that now more than ever. Reaching the top of the mountain and allowing the tearful release of my soul felt good. With a new calm, I go to bed knowing I will climb Camelback each night if I can. And knowing that no matter what happens with Jason I will be okay.

Arizona was the perfect escape, but now that I'm back in Seattle, reality hits. I have two empty apartments to rent, a lot of massage homework and massage exchanges to catch up on, work, and of course physical therapy. I'm never at home. I usually spend the night at Jason's house, nearly 20 miles away, and by the time I return to Bellevue Manor each morning, I have just enough time to head out the door again. Stress from all of my obligations is weighing on me, and those around me, as well.

Jason and I almost break up again. This time because of me, because I don't know what I want. Jason thinks that since we have been together longer than Mark and I had been together, things should be okay. Life should be normal. He doesn't understand that after losing someone you love, life can never be quite normal again. I had hoped he could live with that. But at the end of our most recent argument, I'd asked him to take me home. Fortunately he didn't: instead he listened as I vented and cried and we were able to work things out. Our relationship was renewed and ready for the challenge of the Christmas holiday.

❄

Just two nights ago Jason and I spent the evening decorating for Christmas. Glasses of cabernet in hand, we took bows, popcorn, and lights and quickly transformed our sparse noble fir into an old-fashioned Christmas tree. It was a perfect night, but things have changed.

Guilt for spending so little time with Mark's parents since meeting Jason is heavy on my mind as I drive away from their house and head to Mark's grave. I'd thought I would be a part of their lives. Instead we each have gone on with our separate lives the best we know how. Pulling up to the cemetery, however, I remember that through our love of Mark we will always be connected.

"Mark, I wish you were here with me." I say out loud, as I kneel next to the grave, knees sinking into the wet grass. "I need your help to go on with my life."

I close my eyes and imagine him near me.

"Mark, how do you feel about Jason?" I ask. I want to hear his answer. I know it in my heart, but I want to hear it.

"Will I ever be happy again?" This time the question is for me as much as Mark. I wait for answers but all that come are tears. So many tears that when I finally leave the cemetery and drive to Jason's, they make it difficult to see the highway. Tears that I fear will always be a part of my life.

When Jason sees that I've been crying he puts his arms around me, leads me to the couch, and doesn't let go. When we finally go to bed, my back is so tight Jason gently rocks my legs, which the physical therapist recommends to help the muscles in my back and neck release, until I fall asleep. Sleep I will surely need with a trip to Cashmere planned for the following morning where I will meet Jason's family, on Christmas Eve, Mark's birthday.

Jason and I stop for coffee before leaving town. I had overheard Jason talking on the phone with his brother earlier about playing basketball, so as we hop back into the car I tell Jason that I brought my hightops and I'm ready to play. Jason, looking mostly at his coffee cup, explains that I'm not invited, that I can't play basketball with him and his friends and family. He reasons that it's because he is worried about my safety since I'm not at 100% physically. I know it's because I'm a woman. Of course this concept is not new to me, but not from my boyfriend, not from the person I love.

My blood is boiling and I consider having Jason bring me

back to my car, so I can drive straight to my parents' by myself and skip the stop in Cashmere, but we sit in the parking lot, as cars come and go, and talk it through and then continue on to Cashmere. Jason's parents live up a canyon in Cashmere, home of Aplets and Cotlets, with a picturesque view of the Cascade mountain range. The sun is dipping below its peaks when we arrive and before Jason gives me the tour we admire the sky from the open deck above the pool. His sister Michele and family will be coming in the morning, his brother Russ and wife Sarah are coming later tonight and we expect his parents any minute. But for now, the house is still. When the tour ends in the kitchen Jason lifts my hips onto the kitchen counter. We are eye to eye.

"I'm glad you came with me to Cashmere," Jason says.

I'm glad, too; for now, I will let the basketball incident go. I want to know more about Jason's family and more about him. I had lost that opportunity with Mark; I will not allow it to happen again. Jason sweeps his hand across the side of my face then kisses me hard. I relax my neck. My heart is pounding. Jason unbuttons my Levis and as I lean back and close my eyes I hear the front door squeak. Slipping off the counter, I button up my jeans just as Russ and Sarah pop their heads around the corner and say hello. I flush. I'm mortified, yet thankful it's not Jason's parents.

I don't know his parents but I do know Russ, who also played football at Eastern. And I know I'm in for a crazy evening because Jason and Russ work together like a well-rehearsed comedy show. In fact there was a night in college, where the two of them, who were often mistaken for one another because they look so much alike, sat, guitars in hand, with a large circle of students, mostly girls, gathered around them. They spent the night telling jokes and making up goofy lyrics to old country-western songs. I had spent the night giggling and singing along; I soon realize that things haven't changed.

Sarah, who is relatively new to the Elliott family, welcomes me with her crystal blue eyes. And each time she laughs at Jason and Russ' banter, when her laugh starts from deep in her soul and escapes in her broad smile, I can't help but smile, too.

By the time Jason's parents arrive we have each had several Coors Lights and have begun playing a common Elliott game of tossing grapes across the kitchen for others to catch in their mouths. Jason and Russ are pros. Sarah and I... Well, let's just say we waste a lot of grapes. I haven't been a part of such craziness in a long while and the craziest thing about it is Jason's parents, Bill and Donna, just hop in on the fun. Grape tossing in the Gaubinger house would have been out of the question. It seems as if Jason's parents are disappointed that they have missed the first hour or so of chaos. I love the Elliott exuberance. It is something I'm lacking in my life.

Jason awakens early and puts on his workout clothes and basketball shoes. He walks over and gives me a kiss. I'm under the covers, dying inside.

"J," I say quietly, "I'd really like to play."

"I know, but your arm is not ready and these are a bunch of tough guys," Jason says. "I'm afraid you might get hurt."

"I'd be fine." I say, my stomach beginning to ache.

"Dad and Russ and I will only be gone a couple of hours," he says, "and I just can't bring you, not now. You'll have fun with my mom and Sarah, and Michele should be here soon too. I'll be back before you know it."

I watch him hustle out the door. I can't believe he really did it. Went to play without me. How could he? I feel trapped. If I had my own car I would just drive to my parents and never look back. But I don't, so instead I lay motionless in my bed. Mark would have never done this to me. He knew how important basketball was to me. He would have bragged about me to his friends and family. He would have wanted me on the basketball court. What am I doing here? Just when I think I'm moving ahead in life, life pulls me down again. I've worked hard to be able to play again and then this happens. And all because I'm a girl. Damn it, why shouldn't a woman have the same choices as men?

I try to enjoy my time with Donna, Sarah, and Michele, but the fact that the boys have left me to go play basketball is eating away at me. I have always been one of the boys. Never in my life have I been told to stay with the girls. Of course, I don't like being told to do anything, but missing basketball really stings. I find out the hard way that Cashmere and the Elliotts, which seems to include Jason, are good old boys. Bill is a Cashmere high-school teacher and football coach (and hall-of-fame wresting coach) and Russ is following in his footsteps. Not that these qualifications should make a person sexist, but in combination with a small-town mentality it seems to be more likely. It's difficult to enjoy Jason's family for the remainder of my time in Cashmere. In my heart I know I will have to make a very difficult choice, one that has to do with Jason and any future we might have together. I can't spend my life with someone that doesn't support my love of basketball, especially now that I'm just beginning to play again.

I drive alone, Christmas Eve day, to my parents in Spokane. It's a hard drive. I think about the weekend with Jason's family but most of my thoughts shift to Mark. I wonder what it would have been like to spend a birthday with Mark. How would he have wanted to spend his special day? It's just one more thing we missed doing together. And since I can't be with Mark right now, I'm glad to be alone. I'm glad Jason and I had planned to spend Christmas apart. I will pick him up on my way back to Seattle but tonight it will be good to be with my family.

Christmas Eve is the night the Gaubinger's celebrate Christmas. So Mom, Dad, Putz, Loré, and I gather around the table while Dad makes a toast. We toast those we love that are no longer with us. To Mark, on what would have been his 27th birthday and Uncle Kurt, and the special people, Jason being one of them, that have come into our lives. I lift my glass, with my right arm, and toast each person at the table, looking them in the eye to thank them for all they have given me, then I lift my glass higher and think of Jason. Even after all that has happened over the past two days, I still wish he were here by my side.

When I call Jason the next morning, Christmas morning, our conversation returns to basketball and I find that my hunch was right. My not being invited to play basketball was a sexist thing. "A woman should know her place" was the consensus at the Cashmere gym. I'm grateful to have a family that raised me to have an open mind. But I'm happy to hear that Jason stood up for me, so the next time, if there is a next time in Cashmere, I can play.

Christmas 1992

Dear Mark,

Merry Christmas and happy birthday. I still miss you every day. Thank you for watching out for me. Life will never be the same without you but with your help, I'm finding my way. I know you understand that I can love you and Jason. It's because of you and the strength you have given me, that I am able to go on. I will always love you, Mark.

Love,
Sonya

I hop out of the car, hightops draped over my shoulder, and meet Jason on our way to the gym door. Clasping my fingers around his, I'm ready to hit the court, at a club near Jason's house in Woodinville. I sit on the floor, back against the wall, and lace up my high tops. Jason is already on the court jawin' with the fellas and getting us on a team. He glances my way and rewards me with an exaggerated wink. I laugh and jog out to meet him on the court. Jason and I play basketball for two hours. When I don't hit my man on the long pass, or I miss a left-handed jumper, or I bobble a rebound, I don't care. In the past it would have killed me, but I know what it's like not to play at all. I am on the court, and as much as I hate my weak game, I love playing and it is even better to be playing with Jason.

Driving home I wonder how it can be. How can it be, that I'm playing basketball again, living my life, and having fun, with Mark gone? I shouldn't be having fun, but I am, and as much as I hate to admit it, I even want to have fun now. I look at Jason behind the steering wheel. He scans the road then turns to me with narrowed eyes.

"What?" he asks.

"Nothing."

"What are you thinking about?" he probes, reaching across the car and setting his hand on my thigh.

"Oh, I was just thinking how lucky I am to have found you," I answer.

"That's right, you are," he says, turning back to the road in front of him before squeezing my thigh with a grin.

My lips curl into a smile and I let out a quiet sigh as the pine trees sweep by the window like the last fourteen months of my life.

TIME FOR CHANGE

Fireworks light the Seattle skyline and the Space Needle and though it is a spectacular sight it doesn't matter to me. What matters is that it's a new year. And with a new year comes change. Jason has agreed to go to more counseling with me. Our relationship is stronger but I decide it can only help to see "Ms. Kramer" again. And it's a good thing our relationship is doing better because my body is going to hell. Since Christmas, my hip and arm have been killing me and I'm having trouble sleeping because of pain in my neck and shoulders. Because playing basketball again is so important to me, I have continued physical therapy on my own dime, but with the start of a new year I can schedule more appointments now that my insurance kicks in again. Hopefully with increased physical therapy my body will improve, but even more worrisome to me than the pain are the increasing dizzy spells.

With a studied calm I gaze at the 40-foot-long runway that jets out across the ballroom floor, nearly dividing the room in two, and then look up at the stage and the two cascading stairwells, with no banisters, that descend upon each side. It's my first big runway show since the accident and though the stage is opulent it presents a bit of a challenge. It has to be entered from back stage, in the dark. Center stage is easy, but to enter either side, you hike fourteen feet up to the top of the stairwell in darkness to reach the entrances. The morning rehearsal has been a challenge for everyone. Narrow-heeled mules (I'm not talking the ones that carry tourists up the steep hillsides in Greece, we could have used those; I'm talking stiletto pumps with no straps across the heels to hold them in place) slip from models' toes as they try cautiously to make the descent, chin held high. I have found it difficult to maintain the, "I'm just casually strolling along, take a look at my beautiful red silk gown" look, when I'm thinking, "oh shit; I hope I can make it down this thing without my shoes falling off, turning an ankle, and falling into a heap at the bottom of the runway." Amazingly enough, by the end of rehearsal, the show has gone smoothly and there are no sprained ankles. Now everyone has to pull it together one more time, with all the clothes and accessories, for the show.

I look around the ballroom. Exotic bouquets bursting with color, sit in the center of each table that has been set for at least ten guests and upon each chair sits an adult "goodie bag" filled with treasures. I consider peeking inside but instead return backstage for hair and makeup. I'm thankful that the big shows supply makeup artists and hair stylist. With my arm not up to par it's helpful, plus if I end up with what Bampa calls a "hair don't," it's not of my making and Nordstom can't blame me. I just have to do my job and connect with the audience.

My long blonde hair is parted down the middle and plastered flat against my head. The downfall to my hairstylist theory is that it's difficult to act beautiful on the runway if I hate what they've done to my hair. I feel ugly with my hair slicked down, but at least my smoky eyes and dark red lips will be the focus on stage. I find the rack that has my clothes for the show and tuck my bag out of the way. I have a lot of space, which is rare back stage, and my favorite dresser, which is a godsend.

Dressers ensure that a show progresses smoothly. Buttoning buttons, zipping zippers, snapping snaps, tying shoes, and hanging outfits that they strip from our bodies are only a few things they do once a show begins. And with a show like today's, with more than 30 models, there is bound to be chaos backstage and a greater need for the help. Working through all seven outfits on my rack, I unzip zippers and unbutton buttons and check for matching shoes, readying for the start, and the mere seconds I will have to change between outfits. Switching panty hose, tops, bottoms, hats, jewelry, scarves, shoes and hairstyles with each.

It grows quiet backstage. Thumbing though my cryptic notes from rehearsal, I take a final run through, in my head, envisioning the outfit and music for each. Outfit #1: Enter stage L. Meet Kelle at CF low light, pose, lights up, wait 2nd drums. End runway pose, turn out, C split, end 1½ turn, cross Jonette @ M., exit C, no address. #2

I tape my notes to the clothes rack, and then while buttoning my tweed blazer, I notice Jonette freshening her lipstick and ask to borrow her compact to check my own. We give each other the once over. After scanning for hanging threads, offset collars, flyaway hairs and the like, we enter the dark, directly behind stage, get in line, and wait for the music and our cue.

The music blares and within moments models are exiting the stage. Flying by, jackets and hats in hand and making a beeline to their place in the organized chaos that is beginning to unfold. Just as I reach the top of the stairway and wait for my cue, I feel dizzy. Don't look up or down. Straight ahead, Sōn. Look straight ahead. I stand at the top of the cascading stairwell and, breathing deeply to focus, I wait for my cue to go. When the music fades I get the "go!" I take one slow breath before I hear a second emphatic, "Go!" I step through the black curtain into darkness and my head begins to spin. I glance down, close my eyes briefly then look into the distance before taking my first step. Searching cautiously, I lower my foot, hoping my heel reaches safety below. When it does, my body works on instinct, fighting the vertigo with each step, finding its way to center stage and Kelle. My lips have been drawn in a tight smile, but now as the lights go up and the drums begin to rumble, a smile spreads across my face. I know I can manage the vertigo on the flat runway. Drums roll for a second time. Awakening from our stillness, Kelle and I, twins on the runway, step into the limelight to work the crowd. My limp is gone but with my head still swimming, the battle is not over.

The vertigo gets worse. It follows me everywhere, everyday. I make an appointment to see a neurologist. Dr Mayghem runs a multitude of tests and suggests I see an ENT as well. The new tests show the expected, minimal brain damage. The recommendation is more vestibular PT exercises, stay active, and deal with it.

I do the best I can.

Everything reminds me of Mark. Walking home from my physical therapy, there is a young couple on the street corner kissing and I can see Mark and me. Not Jason and me, Mark and me, and it kills me. Will I ever feel normal again? While sitting in my apartment with another tall stack of bills staring at me, I can't help wonder how I'm supposed to go on. I feel like I'm the only one who remembers Mark, and his role in my life. Amongst the overflowing pile I see the corner of a pink envelope. It's a letter from Honey and Bampa. When I move to the couch to open it, Brianna hops into my lap. I scratch her ears and kiss her on top of the head. Brianna is here for me. When I open the letter, I realize that Honey and Bampa are here for me too, as well as the rest of my friends and my family.

Kirsten and Leslie come to Seattle. At last I will spend some time with my oldest and dearest nerdy friends. And they will have the opportunity to meet Jason. Our dinner at the Pink Door Italian restaurant starts with a bottle of Chianti and continues with the third degree. Kirsten is pretty quiet but Leslie is like a lion protecting her cub. I sip my wine and watch as Jason holds his own under their scrutiny. Leslie and Kirsten are good friends. They don't want to see me get hurt. In short order I can see that Jason meets their approval. I'm glad. Jason puts his arms around them both for a picture. I snap the shot and hope I'm seeing the future. For now, however, I simply look forward to enjoying as much of the spring as possible with Jason by my side.

It's 11:30 p.m. before I get home from massage school. Having class nearly every night and every other weekend is getting old and I still have nearly six months to go. Had I not met Jason, most nights would be like tonight, where I come home, maybe have a cup of tea, and crawl into bed. But it's not the norm for me now; the drive to Woodinville is. I check my machine and there are several messages. One from Kirsten, saying hello; one from Putz and Loré, checking in; one from Mom reminding me that Dad will be in town tomorrow; and one about Bellevue Manor's vacancy.

After turning over in bed for two hours, I pick up the phone and dial Kirsten. It's 4:30 a.m. in New York, but then, she's used to my untimely calls.

"Hi, Kirsten," I say, now on the couch slowly rolling my head, and phone, side to side.

"Hey Sōn, how are ya?"

"I'm alright," I say, finishing with my neck and finding a comfortable spot on the couch, "but my neck is killing me, I can't sleep."

"Really," Kirsten says, not bothering to hold back a tired yawn.

"Yeah, I'm so sick of it. One stupid doctor tried to put me on antidepressants. I was so pissed. If I need antidepressants, it's not for my neck." I pull a yellow throw from off the back of the couch and lay it across Brianna and my chest. "I hate some doctors. Thank god I like Dr. Perry, my orthopedic surgeon, because my surgery to take the rod out of my leg is April 12 in Spokane."

There's another lengthy yawn from the other end of the line.

"I'm not that boring," I say, smiling to myself, "and guess what?"

"You scheduled a boob job at the same time?" Kirsten jabs, knowing that even as a model I shun cosmetic surgery, making an effort to grow old gracefully. And though I looked into cosmetic surgery for my scars early on, now I can't see fixing them either. Perhaps I'd feel differently had my face been badly scarred, but the scars on my face are hardly noticeable anymore.

I shake my head and laugh. I'm glad I called Kirsten, even if she isn't. Kirsten cheers me up. My "guess what?" question for Kirsten was concerning Jason. He wasn't coming to Spokane for my surgery and though I told him I didn't care, I really want him there. I have begun to count on him more and more and it scares me. What would happen if I lost him too? I don't think I could handle more pain. Kirsten helps me forget about the "what if's" and, without knowing, helps me appreciate the "now."

It's Super Bowl Sunday and Jason and I are off to a party. It's a long drive and we chat about school and work until eventually there is an easy silence. I barely notice the sad country twang in the background, but I feel it in my heart. It starts a deep aching I can't control. And then before I know it, tears are streaming down my face.

"You all right, Sōn?" Jason asks, gently rubbing his hand on my leg.

"Yeah," I say, taking a deep breath, not wanting to cry. Not wanting my past to ruin our fun, "I'll be fine."

Jason pulls off the freeway and finds a Starbucks. He gives me a minute alone by going inside to grab lattes. When he returns the red streaks have faded from my face.

"I'm sorry, J," I say, back in control.

Jason doesn't say a word. Instead he gives me a kiss and starts the car.

I'm tired of the emotional chaos. The intensity that can sweep through my body at any moment in time. Life is a roller coaster. I love Jason but I hate myself because of it. It's hard to let go, it's hard to truly enjoy the times when I feel happy. I'm ready to let go of that part of grief, but I'm still not ready to let go of Mark. I look forward to the time when the guilt fades and only happiness remains.

My camera was lost in the accident. I haven't missed it; the events in my life since Mark died haven't been important, not worth pictures. But now, with Jason, there are times I want to remember, times that have meaning. I'm ready to take pictures again.

Jason and I drive to Portland so I can buy a new camera with no sales tax and we can celebrate Valentine's Day. The old Red Lion Hotel is like most of the hotels I've stayed in over the years traveling with basketball; nothing fancy on the outside, but clean. But when Jason opens the door to our room, it's nothing like it on the inside. There is a bottle of champagne and a huge bouquet of red roses topped with heart balloons. Glancing back at Jason, I set down my purse and open the attached card.

Dear Sonya

Roses are red
Violets are blue
It's impossible to explain
How much I love you!

You are the best
You make my world shine.
Will you please be
My Valentine?

I love you with all my heart,

Jason

"I love you too, J," I say, turning to give Jason hug. "I love you too."

Walking into the Seattle Convention Center for the first of two bridal shows this weekend, after hitting the morning sessions of massage school, I'm about ready to drop. It has been a crazy busy week and it doesn't seem to be slowing down. At least Jason and I will be leaving for our cruise shortly; in fact, because we're leaving soon, I plan to stick around Bellevue Manor over the weekend to get caught up on everything.

I toss my bag behind the rack and start looking through my clothes. Since there has been no fitting or rehearsal, I take off my clothes and start trying on the wedding and bridesmaid dresses one by one. They are all do-able until I reach one that stops me dead in my tracks. I pull the dress out from the other dresses and take a long look at the off-the-shoulder V-neck. It can't be. I run my hand down the beaded bodice. But it is. It's my wedding dress. The wedding dress I was supposed to wear when I married Mark. There is a pain in my throat. How can I wear my wedding dress and walk down the convention center's imaginary aisle on someone else's arm? How can I possibly do this and not cry? I put the dress back, I know it will fit. I finish trying on the outfits on my rack and push away all my thoughts and the ache in the pit of my stomach. I take a deep breath, touch up my make up, and put on my first dress and a smile.

After shimmying the narrow blue taffeta bridesmaid's dress down my hips, I step out of it and hand it to my dresser. When I glance at the next dress on the rack, I see my wedding dress. Memories flood my mind. Good and bad. But I push them away as I pull on ivory hose and search for my shoes (the wedding shoes I bought to wear for my wedding), before lifting the crisp white dress over my head. I pull a full slip up under the dress while heading for the long table overflowing with fresh bridal bouquets backstage.

"This one's perfect," says the stout woman with pink stiletto heels as she holds up a fresh arrangement of Calla Lilies and Ivy.

"Yes, it is," I whisper. Calla lilies had been my first choice for my bridal bouquet, but they were expensive to buy in November, so I had opted for Sonia roses.

Tears are not far behind as I step into place backstage but before I have time to think, I receive the "Go." Stepping into the bright lights my body takes over. My "husband" is stage left and with the first cord of Pachelbel's "Canon," we move and come together at center stage. With my arm wrapped in his, we walk down the aisle.

I make it through the show. It's the car ride home that gets me. What are the chances that I would have to wear the dress I was supposed to wear in my wedding. The dress that should be tucked away in my closet for Mark's and my daughter. The dress that should be surrounded with joyous memories. Not the dress that came to haunt me. How can life continue to be so cruel?

227

Life is crazy, and then I really start working. I don't think I will survive. After I'm pegged as one of the models-meeting organizers, Nordstrom quits booking me for shows. But this seemingly bad turn of events means more print work. Shows generally use up a portion of three separate days, with the fitting, the rehearsal, and the show itself. Now with three extra days per week, I'm getting print work to fill the space. Print work that pays more than twice what runway shows do. With the Easy Spirit commercial and more print work I'm actually getting ahead of my bills.

With April showers comes surgery. But before that comes taxes and everything in-between. Monday starts at my accountants. The appointment goes well because I'm getting money back on my taxes. Then I show apartments, and then I work out and do my physical therapy before I go to class all night. I wake up early Tuesday for a Lamont's summer layout photo shoot and wear shorts and tank tops outside in freezing weather. I'm afraid I'm going to cry, my bones ache so. From there, thankfully I drive straight to Moon's to receive a massage; and after my massage, I swing by Mark's grave. Sitting there, body still aching from the long day, I feel old and alone. In the morning I have a photo shoot to get pictures for my book, then I go directly to a photo shoot for Eddie Bauer all afternoon before class all night. Then I head straight to bed because I have a 4:30 a.m. wakeup call.

I don't sleep most of the night because of my neck, so 4:30 a.m. comes early. And now sitting in a freezing RV headed to Port Townsend to spend the day shooting a Bon Marché commercial I'm less than chipper. Fortunately the crew is nice and, once on location, I do my best to ignore dizzy spells exaggerated by fatigue. After shooting all day we're back in Seattle at 8:30 p.m. and then I run to massage class for two hours. The rest of the evening I watch the clock and stretch my neck. It's past 1:00 a.m. when I last check the time. I wake up at 6:00 a.m. to clean the apartment complex, show an apartment and meet with Gordon, my manager.

The evening news is on when I finally relax on the coach, with Brianna in my lap. With the week and all its chaos behind me, I'm ready to pack my bags for our cruise. Once packed, I should go straight to bed, but instead I pull out my journal and write.

April 1993

If I didn't have a break coming with this cruise, I don't know if I could make it. At least Jason and I have been doing well. I love him so much. I know he still doesn't understand my ups and downs, but he tries and that's all I can ask for. I see us together in the future as long as we continue to work at it, but I don't know if I will ever be able to get married. I know it hurts Jason when I say so, but after spending five months planning the perfect wedding and then losing Mark, I just can't think about doing it again. It's hard enough just being in a relationship. I guess this is when I take a deep breath, and realize that I can't change the past. Then I do my damnedest to go on and love the people in my life. It's not easy but, especially with Jason in my life now, I'll try.

Jason and I fly separately to Miami. He's coming from a work conference and I'm content to have a long peaceful flight before I meet him at our hotel. When Jason opens the door to our hotel room and invites me in, I'm at ease. It's as if we are on our honeymoon. And we treat it like one as we slowly remove one another's clothes with the anticipation we should have enjoyed the first time we made love.

The cruise itself is not what either of us would have chosen for a vacation. Yet we have a blast. We climb Dunn's River Falls in Jamaica, sit in a bar in Cancun drinking margaritas (my SoloFlex commercial running in the background) and spend a lot of time at the pool drinking tall colorful drinks adorned with umbrellas. We simply hang out, without the stress of our daily lives. It's as if we are a different couple living a different life. There are times I need a break, when I search for the uninhabited corners of the ship and sit alone looking into the never ending waves and visit the past and the pain that still lurks in every corner of my being. But each time I escape, Jason lets me go and I love him more for it. Each time I return, I'm closer to being whole.

After returning home from the cruise, life is busy, but it doesn't seem as hard. I interview a few more attorneys and though I don't particularly like any of them, I don't stress out about it. I simply make more phone calls. I take my final exams for massage and now our class preps for the state board written and practical exams. I'm closer to receiving my Massage Practitioner license. And though I've been working nearly every day, I feel more at ease. I am, however, still sick and tired of managing Bellevue Manor. But I have no choice but to stay – I have another surgery to pay for.

THE CYCLE OF LIFE

Jason takes time off work and comes to Spokane for my surgery. I'm glad because I'm nervous. This surgery is a lot different then when I had the screw removed from my arm. Dr Perry is removing a rod, which runs the length of my thigh, and two 6 inch x ¾ inch screw like pins, from my femur. This time I'm required to use anesthesia and I don't like it.

"This is a good thing," I remind myself as I lay on my gurney in pre-op.

"You'll be fine," my mom says, "Dr. Perry will take good care of you."

I know it's best to have the rod removed at my age, to give the bone a chance to build calcium, but now I'm wishing I had decided against surgery. My leg is fine.

"It's the right decision, Sonya," Mom says, reading my mind.

"I'll have to be on crutches for a long time," I complain one more time. No more basketball. No more work. No more cleaning the apartment complex. "Jason, can you help me with the apartment complex?"

"Yes," he looks perplexed, "of course."

"I guess this surgery won't be too bad," I say with a smirk, imagining Jason doing my daily chores at Bellevue Manor.

"Get out of here," he says, then leans over to give me a kiss. "I love you," I whisper in his ear. "I really love you, J."

"I love you, too," he says as the nurse rolls me away.

All I remember is puking, a lot of puking. I had anesthesia after my accident, but I don't remember coming out of it. I hadn't expected to feel so terrible, maybe not up and shopping at Nordstrom's like the last surgery, but definitely not this bad. I'm thankful I get to spend the night in the hospital and I'm glad Jason is by my side. He's had two knee surgeries so he understands, but it's more than that, it's good to be with the man I love.

I get off pain killers right away; my biggest problem is slowing down. I'm not supposed to put weight on my leg for one month, otherwise the femur can snap, so I try to take it easy because I want my leg to heal properly. But it's nearly impossible.

The answer became PSPs: Post surgery projects. I plan a bunch of them to keep me busy, along with school and the apartment complex. Some are as simple as better organizing bills and taxes but others take more time and energy. I put a photo album together of Mark and me. I'm glad I finally do it, but it's difficult to look through the pictures realizing that these are the moments that will always be in my memory while many others will eventually slip away. I also start writing my will. Jason and I have really worked things out and I see us spending our lives together. I know what it's like to be left as That Girl and I want Jason to be taken care of if anything happens to me. I want our time together to count, not just for Jason and me, but for everyone. A will is a priority on my PSP list.

Massage is a vessel of healing. Massage school, though difficult at times, even all-consuming, has been good for me.

Not only does it give me something besides my troubles to focus on, it brings focus to my body and its healing. Part of our classwork is to give and receive massages and though it's one more thing on my list of things to do, it brings a healthy balance to my life. Next week our entire massage school is going to Breitenbush Hot Springs, a resort in Oregon, and though I will be missing out on some of the hydrotherapy work (hot tubs and cold plunges) because of my incision from surgery, the emphasis on health and body work will be good for me.

Breitenbush may be good for me, but it sucks. I can't ride bikes and go on hikes like everyone else, I can't go in the water and to top it off the food is nasty vegetarian stuff. Not that vegetarian food is always bad, but whatever spice the cook is using, I don't like, and he uses it in every meal. And I miss Jason. I keep thinking how much fun the resort would be with him here, even with me on crutches. I make the best of it, but I'm eager to go home.

When I get home, however, the Bellevue Manor dumpster is overflowing and the whole area needs to be cleaned. As the apartment manager it is my job (even on crutches) and it's a bad one. When Jason arrives at my apartment I feel like I've been sprayed by a skunk even though I scrubbed in the shower until the water ran cold.

"I'm so sick of this place," I roll my eyes; a musty odor lingers in the air. "I wish I could afford to move out but with the bills from my surgery I really shouldn't."

"You can make it until you leave for Europe," Jason says. "I can help with the cleaning."

"I know, but I also have to clean and rent two units this month. And there's school every night. Then I drive a half an hour to your house after school every night."

I'm sick of it.

Jason is silent.

"It would be a lot easier if I moved into your house," I suggest.

Jason's eyes move around the room, landing any place but on me. "I don't think that's a good idea."

I have no choice but to stay at Bellevue Manor. But still, I wonder why Jason won't even consider having me move in with him. I like that perhaps he feels it is ethically not a good idea unless we are married, but I don't know if I will ever be ready to get married. How can we spend our lives together without living together? Perhaps our future is in question?

May 1992

I looked at moving into an apartment in Lynnwood that cost $350 a month, but it seems ridiculous for me to spend that kind of money for a nice place for Brianna to live. So I've decided to stay at Bellevue Manor. Just a few more months and I'll be done with massage school and it's off to Europe! Just one more week and I'll be off crutches, thank god!

Five pounds in less than a month. That is what sitting around will do for you. I'm not sure it's five pounds since I don't like to step on a scale but I'm getting dimples on my thighs and that is not a good thing, especially as a model. More of a concern than getting out of shape is my lack of exercise for the fun of it. I need exercise, especially basketball, because along with my writing it's a way for me to escape my daily stresses. I struggle to keep my sanity and struggle to stay off my leg.

In fact when I attend Jason's family golf tournament, I temporarily lose it for about two golf swings when I break down and play. Then I make myself put the golf club down for fear of snapping my femur at the next tee, dropping to the grass in a heap and having to start over with my leg in worse shape. So, I watch. And as I watch, I get to know Jason and his family better. Jason, the youngest of three, is a goof-ball, in the best of ways. He makes everyone laugh. Being incapacitated I become the self appointed photographer and bartender, handing out beers from the cooler on our cart. I snap shot after shot of the family and tons of Jim Carrey like close-ups of Jason. He makes me smile.

By the time we are 4 holes in to the round, I realize it's a good thing I'm not playing. First of all, I'm not the best golfer and Jason, his brother, and his dad are the most competitive people I've ever seen. I'm competitive of course, being an athlete, but the Elliott boys harass one another, in a "loving" way, on every stroke, every chip, and every putt, every step of the way. They thrive on it. His grandpa, though not an Elliott, does it too, but in a subtle way. His grandma and his mom, Donna, while competitive, are quiet and unassuming. (Yet they could hit the ball nearly as well as the men.) Sarah, Russ' wife, takes me under her wing. And despite my stressful introduction over the Christmas holiday and not being asked to play basketball, I have grown to enjoy them all in the several times now we have been together. I'm not used to a big family, if you can call the Elliott family a big family. But with Mike and Michele and their kids, Billy, Mikayla and Elliott gathered around us at the 18th hole, it seems like a wild but fun loving mob, compared to mine. A mob that I'm beginning to care about as much as I care about Jason.

I'm going through a lot of changes. I have always considered myself a loner; in fact, except for when I'm playing basketball, I draw energy from being by myself. Since the accident, not only do I need time to myself, a part of me is afraid of getting too close to anyone for fear that I will lose them. I feel closer than ever to Jason and his family. It would be a good time for me to see Ms. Kramer if only I had more money for counseling. But for now, I wait.

I attend my first funeral service ever. It's for Mike Atwood's younger brother. It's difficult to find the right thing to say. It helps me understand why, after Mark was killed, people either kept their distance or said nothing at all. I can only say, "I'm sorry." When I leave I can't stop my tears from flowing.

Grandpa Lowry moves into Northwest hospital. His cancer has returned and he needs full-time care. Mark would have been there daily so I do my best to visit. It's not nearly enough but it's all I can do.

Sitting on the edge of the bed, I clasp Grandpa's slender hand in mine. His skin is buttery soft. I find myself running my fingers along the protruding bones while he drifts in and out. When he is awake I talk with him about what a wonderful man Mark was and how much I miss him.

"I love you, Sonya." he says.

"I love you, too, Grandpa."

I watch his eyes open and close. I think of Mark. I want him here with me, with his grandpa, with his family. I love you too, Grandpa. When Mark died, so did his grandpa's spirit. You'll be with Mark soon.

I can't attend Grandpa's funeral. But I know it isn't necessary: I missed Mark's funeral and that didn't make me love him any less. I know the loss would be harder if he were my Bampa, but I still hurt inside. I try to remember that Grandpa Lowry is no longer in pain and I like to think he is happy now with Mark. And a part of me even wishes I could be with them.

Cadaver class for massage school, though interesting, tests my strength. It's difficult not to look at the lifeless body and think of Mark. Think of what his body might have looked like without its spirit. I'm fine during class, but when I think of it, of him, on my drive home, I have to pull over. I stop at Green Lake and find a bench where I can be alone by the water.

The days become more difficult. There is added stress. I have more back and neck pain, and the skin above my scapula has been going numb. I'm worried it might have been caused by my chipped vertebrae or perhaps a disc problem. I also have eczema covering my arms. I'm falling apart.

I finally receive the go ahead to walk without crutches (though for short stints I had already been doing so). And soon after, I spend four days in Portland doing shows for Nike. I return to Seattle and am bombarded by an answering machine full of messages, almost all of which are from my mom. The first, "Hi, this is your mom; give me a call." The next few are the same, with increasing panic. Then comes the last phone call, where my mom is beside herself, "Sonya, call me. I'm so worried. Please call as soon as you get this message." By the time I listen to the last message, I too, am beside myself. I'm 27 years old. I don't have to report to my mom every time I leave town. I'm also not a mother who almost lost her daughter. So I don't understand.

Putz calls just as I finish the last message. I unload to my big brother about our mom. Putz listens to my complaints and then reminds me that Mom is worried about me. Not long ago she thought she would lose me forever. When I hang up the phone it doesn't seem so bad to have a mom who cares.

There's nothing but sagebrush for miles on our trip to Spokane to visit my family. I peer out the window at the all-too-familiar Eastern Washington terrain and think back to the trip, nearly two years ago, that changed my life. I think of where my life has gone since then and where I want it to go. I think of how lucky I am to be here now with the man I love.

"I know you're not crazy about me going to Europe in the fall. But I have to go. It's something I've been planning for a long time," I say to Jason but sound like I'm trying to convince myself.

"I understand," he says without conviction.

"Maybe we can plan another trip together," I say, looking up the Columbia River as we make the crossing that connects the barren shores, "but I need time alone first."

Jason's quiet and I wonder if I dare bring up another sore subject. But true to my nature I keep talking.

"I saw Janet yesterday," I say.

"You mean Ms. Kramer?" he asks.

"Yes," I answer, my cheeks tightening with a grin. "Anyway, I talked with her about whether or not I would ever want to get married."

"And?" he asks.

"I just don't know if marriage is something I can commit to," I say, wishing I could give him a different answer. "I mean I love you, and I want to spend the rest of my life with you, but I don't know if I can get married, I just don't know if I can go through that whole process again."

Jason is quiet. Maybe he's afraid to say the wrong thing or maybe he doesn't have anything to say. I just want to crawl under a rock and cry.

"I love you, Sōn," he finally says. "Let's not worry about marriage right now."

I give him a kiss on his cheek, rest my hand on his thigh and melt into the passenger seat.

EVENING OF GRACE

I need a break. I can't stand life anymore. I can't stand myself. The two-year anniversary of the accident, of Mark's death, is coming up. The wind, the grass, and the sky all remind me of him. Everything reminds me of him, or should I say losing him. I'm a wreck emotionally and physically. I have spent over a month on crutches and just as I'm beginning to get stronger again, I fall ill and spend three days sick in bed. I am going crazy.

I've been staying with Jason even more. After spending the afternoon cleaning up his house I realize it is starting to feel like my home, especially with the red roses that Jason brought home for me, for no particular reason, that are sitting on the dining room table. Although Jason's home is starting to feel like my home, still a part of me needs to get away. I pull out the yellow pages and make several calls.

Jason's in his office in the basement. My hip is stiff, so I hug the rail on my way down to see him.

"Hi, J," I say sneaking up behind him as he sits at his desk doing paperwork.

"How ya' doin'?" he asks, standing up to give me a hug.

"Pretty good." I answer, burrowing my face into his chest.

I stay this way for as long as I can, then lean back against his grey file cabinet. He looks sharp in his suit and I almost feel bad for wrinkling his crisp white shirt, but I feel worse for what I am about to say.

"J," I start out slowly, wondering if I should cancel the reservation even though I know it is what I need. "I think I need to be by myself this weekend."

Jason's face drains, then recovers. "Okay," he says, working to sound supportive. "That's fine."

"It'll be two years since the accident and I need to be alone."

I feel like I just slapped him across the face. He nods, trying his best to understand.

"I found a cabin at Mount Rainer that is really cheap," I say, glancing at my now clammy hands. "I rented it for a couple of nights."

"That'll be good for you," Jason answers, sitting back down at his desk.

I lean down and give him another hug, squeezing him hard now that my right arm is getting stronger and finishing off his once crisp, white shirt.

"Thank you, J."

I can feel the tension that's been building over the past months escape with every mile and every tear. The tears are all but gone by the time I reach the gravel drive that leads to the long row of cabins in Mount Rainier National park. Rustic log cabins would have been my preference. These are not rustic; they are simple reddish-brown wood boxes, set side by side, but they are far from Seattle and far from everything that, right now, seems overwhelming in my life.

After checking in, I park next to my assigned cabin. The cabin is small. There is a tiny standing fireplace and a queen sized bed that takes up the rest of the room and a bathroom smaller than the one in my apartment. Fortunately I don't have much to unload, but there is one box in particular that seems heavy, because it weighs heavy on my heart. It is a box filled with Mark; pictures of Mark, cards from Mark, journals about Mark. I brought it knowing I had to go back there, back to a time when my life was very different. I squeeze the box between the wood paneling and the polyester floral bed spread and onto the floor, to look at later. When I lower myself to the bed and lie down, I am relieved to feel a firm mattress under my back and grateful that when I close my eyes and relax, I see Jason.

After a short nap, I gather myself and head to the mountain. There is something in nature that for me helps relieve tension, and at the same time helps me feel closer to Mark, especially high on a mountain. My dad has climbed Mt. Rainer many times and on his 40th birthday he took my brother along. Maybe that's why I'm drawn to the mountain, to nature. It's in my blood. The love of nature, of fresh air and pine trees, is a part of who I am. But I won't attempt to summit Mt. Rainier today; a simple hike is all I have in mind. When I reach the lodge at Paradise, I notice the snow pack seems low enough for me to reach with a short hike, so I head up the nearest trail.

When I reach the snow there are two young snowboarders practicing jumps. They have hiked up with their boards and built themselves a ramp. I make a miniature snowman out of snowballs, take a self portrait with the timer on my camera, and then find a dry rock where I can watch the snowboarders from a distance. I think of Mark. He has been gone, dead, for two whole years. It has been two years since I held his face in my hands and kissed his lips. Two years since we held one another tight and made love. The what-ifs, are unthinkable, especially when I think of children. How many great things we would have done together. Swallowing hard, I lower my face to my knees and cry. When I look up the snowboarders have gone and I am alone. The tears have washed through the depths of my soul and I sit in silence as the sun moves low in the sky. When I begin my slow descent down the trail, I am at peace.

A roaring fire fills the small cabin. Once in my flannel jammies, I'm ready to tackle the box that's squeezed alongside the bed. I reach down and pull out the box, Mark's box. I carefully take off the lid. Sulfur from our wedding matches, gold and black inscribed with Our Life, Our Beginning, Sonya and Mark, November 8th, 1991 wafts out of the box. I pull out a slender packet and hold it to my nose. I am tired of the tears, but they come anyway, and this time I don't fight them. Why should I? I look again. A card catches my eye. The storks with high tops on and a heart above their heads may look silly but the words are haunting. *You will never know exactly how much you mean to me and how deep my love is for you...* I close the card, set it down and reach for the next. And this is how the evening progresses as one by one I empty the box of cards, and movie tickets, and basketball tickets, and poems, and photos and Mark's driver's license and business card, and every bit of Mark that I have, that I will ever have. I remove them all from the box and set them around me on the bed. I take it all in and allow the pain in my heart to spread throughout my body. And as it does, I think I might die from the pain. But I don't, and by the next morning I am ready to start the day. And when my stay at the cabin is over, I hope that I will be ready to go on, ready to truly live my life.

I wait patiently in my car for the evening ferry to begin unloading at the Mukilteo terminal just outside Everett. My commercial shoot in Port Townsend ran late and I'm bummed that I missed the earlier ferry because Jason is driving up from Woodinville to meet me at The Ranch, a country western bar in Everett, and I am late.

So much has changed in my relationship with Jason. In the beginning, I kept our relationship hidden. Not wanting to go out in public for fear of what Mark's friends or family might think if they saw us together. My guilt has been an added burden to my pain. As much as I want to change the way I feel, I can't. I have apologized again and again to Jason, but somehow he didn't need apologies, he understood. So without pressure or promises, we have become a couple. It hasn't been easy but we are together.

When I arrive in Everett I find the bar, which is only blocks from where Mark grew up and is now buried, and park my car. Jason is waiting patiently in the lobby. When he sees me, he walks over and pulls me close, greeting me with a smile and a gentle kiss.

We dance all night. Fortunately, it is relatively easy for me to line dance and, more importantly, slow dance. I hate for the evening to end, and though it would have been nice to drive back to Seattle together in one car, I had planned to stop by Mark's grave, so it is best that we are driving separate cars. It's been a while since I have made the trip to Mark's grave and tonight, I need to go.

"J, I think I'm going to stop by Mark's grave on the way home."

"Would it be okay if I came too?" he asks.

"Sure," I say, before I have a chance to question my decision.

Jason and I stop at the nearest grocery store and I settle on a dozen red roses instead of a dozen Sonia roses, like I'd hoped. We climb back into separate cars and I drive through the brick entry of the cemetery with Jason close behind. A single dim lamppost shines in the far corner, but the moonlight breaks through the darkness with just enough light that we can easily make our way to Mark's grave and read the gravestone. I park and look out at the rhododendron just to the left of Mark's grave; Jason pulls in behind me and stops. Grabbing the roses I take a deep breath and step out of my car. Jason walks up behind me and holds my free hand, somehow knowing just what I need.

We follow the flat gravestones like a path, passing the spot where Mark's grandfather is buried, until we come to rest in front of Mark's gravestone.

Jason and I stand together in silence. Tears well in my eyes and when my lower lids are full, the tears begin to spill onto my cheeks. My grip on Jason's hand tightens. I take a long deep breath to maintain my composure.

We stand, silent. Squeezing Jason's hand, I finally kneel to the ground and put the roses in the vase. Jason follows me and we stay, on our knees, holding hands for quite some time. Eventually, we lie on our backs and look up at the star filled sky. Side by side on Mark's grave.

"What was Mark like?" Jason asks.

I take another deep breath and let it slowly escape from my mouth, unsure of how I should answer. Then I give a lengthy answer no boyfriend or lover would want to hear. An uncensored description of the man I loved so dearly and after this night a man to whom I would have to learn to say good-bye. Jason asks about Mark until the night grows cold and the closeness of our bodies can no longer keep us warm. The stories spill from my body, one by one, finally giving way to my pent up sorrow. Jason pulls me against his chest and holds me while I cry. It is at this moment, I remember the prophetic words spoken by Mark not so long ago. "Don't let a good thing go," Mark had said. He was right, although my relationship with Jason may have come too soon and at a time that is very difficult for us both. What Mark had said rings as true now as it had then. I need to hold on to Jason. I have found another man who loves me. Now I need to slowly let go of the past and find a way to return that love.

A FALLEN SOUL

I love Jason. But if I think about marrying him, I feel sick to my stomach. I'm not ready to go there yet – marriage. I think living together is the answer. It would be a good test for us and I hate to admit it, but it is also the perfect solution to get me out of Bellevue Manor. Not terribly romantic, but true. It doesn't matter, however, because Jason still won't have anything to do with the idea. And his parents are dead set against it, as well.

"You're 25 years old," I argue, nearly ready to give up. "It's your decision, not your mom's."

"I don't think we should move in together."

"Jason," my voice grows louder, "what if I never want to get married? I don't know if I can go through that again." I'm holding back tears.

Jason is quiet.

"I want to be with you Jason. And I know it doesn't seem like the right reason, but we spend almost every night together anyway, and I have to drive back and forth and manage this stupid apartment complex. I'll be leaving for Munich after massage school is over, anyway. We could have a trial run for a month or so."

"I don't know, Sōn."

The world has been lifted from my shoulders. Well, at least Bellevue Manor, but it feels like the world. Jason decided we should give it a try, living together. I'm not sure what changed his mind. Perhaps he realized it might be our only future or perhaps he just wanted us to be able to snuggle together every night. Whatever the case, I'm pleased and a bit relieved. He has even agreed to keep Brianna when I travel to Munich, which is probably a bigger leap for him than us living together.

Once moved in, with permission from Jason and his roommate, I pull down the college posters and quarantine them to the basement. Together we paint the pale walls bright white, add my furniture and make Jason and his roommate's house my home, too.

With a month of school left and State Boards still to pass, I really appreciate my new home. But more than anything, I appreciate Jason. He's made a lot of sacrifices for me; the biggest, and one I can never change, is he will never experience the carefree and giddy stage of being new lovers with me. I can only hope we have something better, something that will last. A loving relationship built with hard work and understanding.

Jason is so helpful, simply by listening. Listening as I complain about my aches and pains, especially my neck that still keeps me up at night, listening as I study for my massage boards, that also keeps me up at night and listening as I struggle through interview after interview with attorneys, hoping to find someone who will take care of my case, with my best interest in mind, and end the added burden of my ongoing lawsuit.

Jason's presence brings me strength.

I throw a stack of attorney's brochures on the kitchen table. I'm tired of it all and would simply wash my hands of the case if my medical bills weren't continuing to mount. The next day I drive an hour to Mt. Vernon to see yet another attorney.

Paul Luvera's office accepts my case. Paul Luvera and Ralph Brindley are professional and more important, likeable. They seem honest. They explain that Mark can not be discussed in the lawsuit, which I already knew. They explain that since I can walk and I look good, we don't want to go to court, to sit in front of a jury. They advise me to go on with my life while they work toward a settlement. I lean back and sink into the soft leather chair. I know I'm at the right place.

A toast is in order. I have a new attorney and my massage boards are behind me. I'm ready to celebrate, even without the test results.

"J, I'm home," I holler as I step through the front door.

A muffled "down here" drifts up from the basement and there is a bounce in my step as I descend the stairs to his office. Peeking in the door I present a broad smile.

"I did it," I say.

"How'd it go?" Jason asks, turning in his office chair and patting his hands on his thighs.

"Good, I think," I say, plopping my derrière in his lap.

"When will you know if you passed?" he asks.

"A couple months," I take a deep breath and let it out, "I'm just glad it's over."

"Let's celebrate," Jason says, then pushing me up off his lap, adds. "Let me finish here and then I'll take you to dinner."

I lean over and gave him a huge hug and as I turn to walk away he smacks my behind.

"Watch it," I say with a scowl, before I head upstairs to change for dinner.

With one wine bottle empty we order another. Lucca's is one of the two restaurants we frequent in Woodinville. The first is Azteca, for their margaritas, and the other is Lucca's, our hole-in-the-wall spot, were we can get a nice bottle of wine with pasta without robbing a bank. I love the cozy setting. Painted grapevines wrap around the room and climb on to the tablecloths. Small votive candles sit on every table, each with a single rose placed in slender crystal vase. With my stomach full of chicken parmegiana, I push my plate to the side and focus on the wine and Jason. When the second bottle of cabernet arrives, we start on our crème brulée. Jason's eyes are lazy, comforting. When he reaches across the table and runs his finger gently between my index and middle finger, it sends shivers through my body. His touch lingers between the next two fingers, then the next, before he slips his hand into mine. With his attention on our hands he hesitates before he looks up and when his lips part, my heart flutters.

"I can't believe you're leaving next week," he says. He reaches his other hand across the table and takes both my hands.

"I know," I say, my heart settling as I look down at our clasped hands. Had I really just hoped for Jason's proposal? I push the thought away.

It is quiet.

"I've been planning this trip for a long time," I say, biting my lip. "It's something I need to do."

Now more than ever, I wonder why I insist on traveling to Munich on my own. At one time, it had given me something to look forward to, but maybe with Jason as a part of my life, I don't need to go. Or do I? Mark still occupied my mind. His memories, although not as alive as they used to be, reside right next to thoughts of Jason. I need the time away in Munich. I need the time alone.

Jason doesn't say a word; instead he gently rubs his thumbs across my hands. Over the past week a heavy weight has been lifted from my shoulders, but now as I gaze across at the man I love, the man I will soon leave, sorrow creeps into my soul.

A FINAL GOODBYE

Jason's cologne lingers in my hair, holding a part of him near me. I turn and look up the tunnel entrance of Gate 4 where Jason and I had kissed one another and said our goodbyes and where he still stands. I wave one last time and then Jason disappears as I enter the cabin of the 747.

Settling into my seat, the drone of the engines numbs my heart and mind. I put on earphones and allow the fluid voice of Natalie Cole to fill the growing void. From my window seat, I watch a black bag with a bright red X be tossed onto the loading belt, then a large green Adidas duffle, then another plain black bag and with each toss, tears form. Leaving is what I wanted, what I had insisted upon. I needed to go alone, needed some distance, some time to think. With me gone, Jason might even change his mind about me, realize I am carrying too much baggage, end it, end us, before our relationship becomes too complicated. It would be easier to have him break up with me now before I open every last bit of my heart to him. I continue to stare out the widow as the plane taxis down the runway and finally leaves the ground.

It's bitter cold when I arrive in Munich as is my heart as I try to forget my life in Seattle. I should have expected it to be cold in Germany in October, but my body isn't ready for the change and it makes my joints ache. My thickest coat doesn't break the chill as I step out of the airport corridor to catch a bus into the city. I exchange traveler's checks for Deutschmarks, buy a phone card, find a phone booth, and take out my Forbes travel guide, all the while wishing I had bundled for Antarctica. I call several possible inexpensive pensions and youth hostels on my search for a temporary place to stay. It's my hope that when I find a modeling agency to represent me in Munich, the agency will have a hotel or apartment, for the models, that will be more affordable. With a short bus ride, I arrive in the city and in minutes I am opening the door to my room. The small rented room is stark, but clean, and the crisp white sheets and duvet invite me in from the cold. The large window, with dark stained oak framing, looks onto Konigsplatz, were no cars are allowed and where this evening it looks as if no people are allowed either.

Day is about to turn to night when I venture out into the cold again for a quick bite and find a small shop that smells like home, the home I grew up in. I ease the effects of the weather with a hot bowl of wurstle mit saft, a German-style hot dog, swimming in goulasch soup and spatzle (dumpling noodles). A young couple in the corner exchange kisses and I have to turn my head and close my eyes. I think of Jason's and my last kiss at the airport. What was he thinking when we said good-bye? Does he wonder if I really love him? I do love him, of that I am sure. I love Mark, but I love Jason, too. I look down at my bowl while I finish dinner then return to my room and crawl into bed, exhausted.

I awaken to a bustle on the streets below and as I peer out the window this time, a speck of sunlight pokes through the grey sky, freshening the day. After a good night's sleep, the idea of cold-calling modeling agencies seems a little less daunting. I have the names of a few agencies recommended

252

to me by my agency (none of which had been interested when Seattle Models Guild had faxed my composite card) but things can change when you are on an agency's doorstep; plus, I have the names of a few smaller agencies, as well.

Walking down the cool hall, towel and dock kit in hand after a lukewarm shower in the shared bathroom, my leg is stiff. I almost limp up to the sink in my room and I am standing in front of the mirror, toothbrush in hand, when I feel Mark. I feel him there beside me, perhaps trying to let me know everything is going to be okay. I look into the mirror, into my sullen eyes, and wonder what I am doing here. Had the accident never happened, I would have been with Mark, happily married. Now look at me. I look down, past my knobby knees that stick out from beneath the towel, to my pale blue flipflops. I'm standing, goosebumps and all, on a grout-stained tile floor in Munich. And I am all alone. Why am I here?

I pull out a wrinkled black skirt and forest green sweater and do my best to hand iron them on the firm bed. I dig through my backpack for black pumps and black hose but instead pull out a picture of Jason. I framed it just before leaving Seattle. In the shot, Jason's lips are holding back a smile that instead, leaps from his eyes. He's up to no good, is what I'd think if he were a child in the picture.

I bring the picture to my lips.

"I love you, J," I say aloud.

I set the frame on the bedside table, looking one last time before I gather my clothes from the bed.

I love you, J.

Properly outfitted for the day, I write down a tentative schedule. Begging modeling agencies to represent me is not a task I enjoy, especially considering my book is not strong. I have a few new shots in my portfolio, but I'm not crazy about them. And I'm sure most agencies will feel the same. I'm banking on commercial potential; if I can get in to see some agencies, they might see my potential.

I begin the journey of "no's." I start with the top agencies, set appointments and out of necessity begin touring the city. I watch as each agent fans through my book and listen as they give me the honest truth. I am not what they need. I am too big. I am old. My scars are a problem. My book is not strong. I have heard it all before, but day by day it takes a toll on my being. And by day three I'm ready to call it quits.

I take out my journal and begin to write:

I've really enjoyed my walks in the beautiful parks and I love the city center, but I'm not sure what to do. I'm hoping I can get a smaller agency to represent me, to take a chance, but if not.... Maybe I'll go visit cousin Kurti in Austria, a little sooner than expected, do some touristy stuff and then head home early? I don't know.

I'd feel like I was giving up, but I'm not sure why I'm even here anymore. I needed my space to be alone and think about Mark, but now that I'm gone I really miss Jason. I still don't know if I should be in such a serious relationship, but I'm not sure how to stop it either. I don't know. I feel really lost right now and I hate it.

It's like walking onto the court for a big game; I take a deep breath and let it out slowly to relax. My ego has taken a beating and as I walk the rocky path that leads to the front door of Klages Models, I feel a note of confidence in knowing what to expect in response to my visit. Klages Models is a smaller agency, and the moment I step through the door the faces of composite cards that line the wall seem to welcome me rather than look down on me. The slender woman at the front desk with straight, dark hair and round eyes peeks up, phone tucked into her chin, and gestures to the covered red chairs that surround the small coffee table. I take a seat with my Seattle Models Guild book in my lap and wait. Once the woman's off the phone I smile in her direction and receive a smile in return.

"Hallo," comes a welcome, with a familiar accent. "May I help you?"

"Yes," I reply raising up and walking over to the counter where she stands.

"My name is Sonya Gaubinger," I say, awkwardly reaching out my right hand to meet hers across her desk. "I'm planning to be in Munich for several months and I am looking for an agency to represent me."

"I'm Brigitte," she answers and looks at the book under my arm. "May I take a look?"

I hand over the 9" x 11" black book and look on with concern. Brigitte sits down at her desk and opens to the first shot. In the shot, I'm leaning into the camera, with my long hair straight and pushed back across my shoulders, my face is the focus, and I'm wearing a simple black top that is set off by a blue background. It is my favorite shot, really the only good one. My eyes seem to draw you in. None of my other shots really do this. Sometimes with my other shots, I wonder if the camera searches out the sadness and pulls it to the surface, leaving a picture that is somehow unsatisfactory. Brigitte turns the page after she's given the first shot consideration. The pace quickens, she turns to the next, then the next and the next. She quickly makes her assessment.

"I like this shot," she points to the first, and then opens to one near the back, "and this one isn't bad. But you need some new pictures."

I nod in agreement. My heart is racing.

"How tall are you?"

"Five, nine."

"You know that in meters?"

"No."

She mumbles in German, then thumbs through her desk and looks at a small paper.

"Are you sure?"

"Yes," I answer, trying not to sound offended but knowing full well I've lost almost an inch from my accident.

"Hm...what size do you wear?"

"Six, eight"

"Let's measure."

Brigitte opens her drawer again and this time pulls out a measuring tape. I walk around the side of the desk and lift my arms hoping this is all a good sign, but knowing with my boy body my waist measurement is always bigger than a client or agent wants to hear. There is that look again. How can this girl's waist be that big, she doesn't look that big? She measures my hips and bust, and then gives me another look.

"We can try to find you some commercial work. Maybe you could go to Vienna and see some clients there; it's a different market."

"That sounds great," I answer thinking a trip to Austria, my dad's homeland, sounds perfect.

"You'll need to get some new shots for your book," she continues not letting me off the hook that easy, "It needs a lot of work."

"I know," I answer, almost ashamed that she's agreed to represent me, but very thankful.

"Do you know of a good place to stay?"

"Yes, there is a hotel that many of the models stay in. Let me write down the number for you and you can call to see if they have a room."

"Thanks."

"Come in Tomorrow at 9:00 a.m. and I will send you to see clients."

"Great," I reach for my book, then smile one last time. "Danke shön."

I'm lucky. Not only have I found an agency, I have a cheap, clean, place to stay. But instead of staying with another model, I'm rooming with an eccentric, 70-year-old widow, Elsa. She's in town displaying her paintings in galleries and attending the show of a fellow artist. She has more pizzazz than any wannabe model one quarter her age. We brake bread and share stories for breakfast and dinner whenever we are both in the flat. She is a breath of fresh air to my long days of taking buses and trains to every corner of Munich.

She listens to me talk about Mark and Jason and shares her wisdom without even knowing it. I see her happiness, I feel her energy. I wonder where it comes from and how she can go on with such enthusiasm for life after losing her husband of more than 50 years. I come to understand the depth of her energy, her passion for her painting. I cherish every moment we spend together.

Elsa and I part a week later, I to Vienna and she to Switzerland. I arrange with the hotel to return in ten days, and then pack up my things. An hour later I'm boarding a train to Austria.

The tall buildings fade into the distance and it's not long before they are replaced by Bavarian chalets. I prop my right leg up on my backpack, lean back in my seat and close my eyes. It's nice to have the train compartment to myself, though Jason would love this. He would be bouncing all over the place. "Look at how beautiful this is," he would say. "We should've stopped in that town. Did you see the city center? It's so festive." Like a kid in a candy store, that one. I would have just smiled and agreed. Mark would have liked it too. They were more alike than different. I have never allowed myself to think about it before but they would have really liked one another.

"What do you think, Mark?" I look up and whisper.

Mark would have loved Jason. I reach into my bag, grab my journal and write.

Vienna is awful. I thought Munich was cold. Even after buying a warmer coat and some sensible shoes, I freeze on my way to every casting. It's grey and dark and I'm growing bitter. The clients I meet must feel the same, because there are no smiles or enthusiasm from either party. On my last night in Vienna I happen upon a cozy restaurant with an entrance just below street level. I bend down and look in at the tables. Red-and-white checked tablecloths with votive candles carefully placed in the center of each. I walk down the stairway and ask for a table. I order a bowl of goulash soup and some tea. It's all I can afford and all I need. After sitting for a few minutes a man with a hard black guitar case walks in the door. I watch him go to the front desk. He speaks for a moment to the woman who seated me, then walks to the corner near the front window and takes out his guitar. When he begins to play I realize I have found paradise in the midst of a frozen hell, I only wish Jason were by my side.

Back in Munich, Brigitte is not happy. I've returned early and she has not heard any good news. I'm not surprised, but it doesn't matter because I've decided to stay in Munich one more week, visit family in Austria, and then return to Seattle. There I can work and there I can be with Jason. If he still wants me.

When I spot cousin Kurti's beaming smile high above the heads of those waiting in front of him at the train station, I smile. He is leaning, with arms crossed, against the rod iron lamp post. As the train crawls to a stop, I grab my bag and hustle to the door. I'm eager to hop onto the landing and into the arms of family.

"Grüsstig, Sonya," Kurti says in unison with my hello.

I drop my bag for a welcome hug and when I finally let go we are both in tears. It's been a long time since we've seen one another, and the last time, Uncle Kurt and Mark were still alive. There are reasons for tears.

"It's so good to see you, Kurti"

Kurti lifts my bag as if it were empty, gives me one last squeeze with his free arm and then motions to the exit.

We spend the long weekend together. It's nice to see Tante Maria and my two other cousins, Brigitte and Ingrid, but it's Kurti I'm closest to, in age as well as in spirit. We spend our time together touring the area and enjoying a drop of wine or two at neighborhood Mosthauses. Kurti's girlfriend joins us, and though I love being with them, it makes me sad that Jason is not here too. And their relationship reminds me of what Jason has missed by falling in love with me. An experience where both parties jump in with all their hearts, where they know they can't live without one another. An experience like Kurti and his girl friend are sharing and one like I shared with Mark. One without all the bullshit. Jason and I will never have that. And as Kurti leans across his shoulder to give his girlfriend a kiss I wonder if it's fair. I wonder if perhaps I should let Jason go.

After a long goodbye at the station, I hop on the train back to Munich and am quickly mesmerized by the lush green of the Bavarian high meadows. The constant clacking of the wheels against the tracks is calming, and as I wade through layers of sadness and guilt and search for that part of me that has been missing since Mark's death I realize that I have been forging a road to happiness for some time. I have been taking small steps to heal and grow stronger, bringing me to this pivotal point in my life, a million miles from home.

Jason is my knight in shining armor, but that is a problem. Do I deserve to find someone this incredible again and how can I ever give of myself so fully just to have it all torn away? I open up my journal and begin to write.

Nov. 8th, 1993

I'm on my way back to Munich after visiting Kurti and family in Austria. It wasn't until just now when I wrote the date that I realized that it was 2 years ago Mark and I were to be married. It came as a shock to look at the date and remember back to a time that seems so far away, yet in a breath feels like yesterday. Tears flood my eyes when I think of Mark and think back to all I've been through.

I realize, now more than ever, that my life has changed. It will never be the same, but once again I'm sharing my life and my love with someone very special. It's good for me to miss Jason, to feel a little homesick; it helps me see that he is right for me. That I love him and I don't want to lose what we have together. And I also realize (whether it's good or bad, I don't know) that always is a very difficult word to use, because death can change things. But, I believe we will be together. And on this day, the day I was supposed to marry Mark, a day that was supposed to be so special 2 years ago, it is good to know in my heart that I want to marry again, not really again but I want to be married and I am not afraid. I know it will be difficult and it will take a lot of strength by me and understanding by Jason, but I know it will be.

Life is very good. Life is so worth living, especially if

you have someone to share it with.

Jason, I love you!

I set my journal in my lap and look at the sky. The sky is blue with patches of dark clouds that rise to the heavens. I look up at them and feel a presence. I know I'm not alone. I open my journal and continue.

Dear Mark,

I'm writing to thank you for all of your help over the past two years. I know you've been by my side, watching me struggle through this thing called grief.

Death was new to me. I had never lost anyone before you, and to have you torn away so unexpectantly killed me inside. The loneliness has been unbearable. Even when surrounded by people, I've felt alone until now.

Somehow, I've begun to fit in again, to actually feel alive. I know it's what you would have wanted and somewhere deep inside I've begun to think that it's what I want too.

Mark, I love you so much. I'm not sure if I will be able to do this, but it's time for me to really say goodbye. I've said goodbye many times, but now I need to put it in writing.

It doesn't mean I won't think of you, because you are a part of me and always will be. But as hard as it will be to go on without you, I have no choice. Goodbye Mark, I will always love you.

You're forever in my heart,

Love,

Sonya

Drenched in tears, I set my journal in my lap and close my eyes. My body is still, except for the rise and fall of my chest. I sit in silence, waiting for the ache in my heart to subside, waiting to feel normal again. Finally, I lean back and memories come rushing back while my heart becomes lost in the rhythm of the tracks. I see Mark and me on the basketball court, I see us at baseball games, having dinner, making love. I see us, on the movie screen in my mind, more vivid than we have been in a long time. I remember the times, since then. The pain of grief and the long, sometimes unbearable road of recovery. But then I think of how I have managed that road, and I think of Jason. I see how he has helped me move through this hard time. How he has stayed by my side, even when I didn't know what I wanted, when I kept pushing him away. I see him now, as if he were beside me and realize he could be beside me right now. He is my life, my future, and I finally really see it. No, I feel it. I know it's what I want, what I need. As the train nears Munich, there's a different ache in my heart. My heart aches for Jason. For him to know I am ready to go on with my life. I am ready to marry Jason, to be with him, with all my heart and soul, for the rest of our lives.

EPILOGUE

Jason and I stroll hand in hand up Sixth Avenue. It's 3:00AM and the commotion of Seattle's New Year's festivities has faded. An early morning mist settles beneath each lamppost we pass. My mind is at peace this New Year. Our dinner at Dukes and the long walk on the docks and shores of Lake Union has been the ideal ending to 1993. Basking in the comfortable silence, the air crisp against my warm cheeks, I lean my face into Jason's shoulder. Jason kisses the top of my head and my body relaxes into his as we meander up the sidewalk toward our car. Suddenly Jason stops and pulls me close. Then he steps back and, holding both my hands, he narrows his eyes and his face grows serious.

"I love you, Sonya," he says, his eyes now searching mine.

"I love you too," I say. Meaning it with every inch of my soul.

"Sonya?" Jason takes a long slow breath in and lets it escape. His eyes begin to sparkle just before his lips break into a wide smile. "Sonya, will you marry me?"

My heart stops. We had enjoyed an incredible evening but I hadn't expected a proposal, but there was no question of my reply.

"Yes Jason, I would love to marry you!"

I can't believe that life came full circle. I found someone

that I loved as much as I had loved Mark, someone with whom I can share my life. Of course I am scared. I have suffered the pain of loss once and there is no guarantee that Jason and I will be together forever, but I'm ready to give life a chance again.

Jason and I spend the winter and spring of 1994 backpacking in Europe and then return to Seattle to plan a wedding. Our wedding day is a flurry of activity. First much of the wedding party, including myself, attends a high school football jamboree where Jason, his brother Russ and Dad are coaching. I leave early to help my family prepare the reception hall. In the afternoon I take time alone to get ready for the wedding. I think about everything that has happened over the past 3 years. I think of Mark, and how I wish he had never died, how I wish life hadn't taken so many of us that loved him down that painful road, but most of all I think of Jason and how lucky I am to have him in my life. After putting on a light coat of matte mauve lipstick, I open the bag that holds my wedding dress only to find that there is no slip. The bridal salon had forgotten to pack the full slip that makes my dress complete. With hot rollers bouncing on top of my head, I search downtown Seattle for a slip. My chest tightens and tears creep into my eyes as I come up empty handed at every store. Finally, I stop, take a deep breath, and remind myself of what is really important. It doesn't matter if my dress sags, or if I have a wedding dress at all, what matters is that I have Jason by my side.

Jason and I marry at the Fauntleroy Church in West Seattle, September 3, 1994. As the sun comes up the following morning we drive to a local high school gym and meet friends and family. We gather to play basketball. Playing basketball with Jason, and all the people I love, is the best honeymoon I can ask for. And it's the perfect beginning to Jason's and my future together as man and wife.

Sonya playing basketball in college

Sonya and Mark at his sister's wedding

Sonya and Mark goofing around on a softball tournament roadtrip

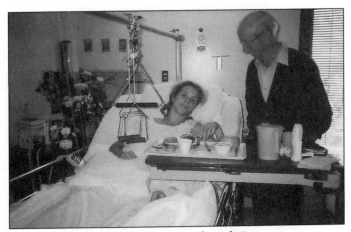

Sonya in the Hospital with Bampa

Sonya and her dad go for a walk

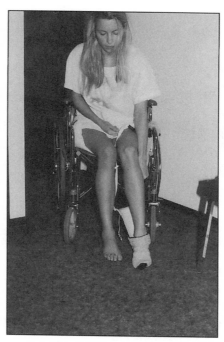

Sonya works to put a sock on by herself

Mark's grave

Sonya and Jason New Years Eve

The Elliott Family 2009
(Charli, Sonya, Jason, Cass and boxer dog Sassy)

SONYA ELLIOTT is a writer, a basketball coach, a fashion model and a mom. She is the owner of Full Court Design and founder of the PeaceLoveBasketball organization. Both support today's youth through her love of the game and love of life. An all-conference academic basketball player, Sonya attended Eastern Washington University on an athletic scholarship and graduated with honors. Along with coaching, Sonya continues to play basketball competitively in Seattle's top women's leagues. She is married and has two children.

ACKNOWLEDGMENTS:

It's hard to know where to begin. Do I start with those who literally saved my life or those who continue to make my life worth living? There are so many that made this book possible but first and foremost I have to thank my family for supporting me every step of the way.

To my husband Jason, my teammate for life, thank you so much for understanding me, comforting me, putting up with me, making me smile and, most important of all, loving me for who I am. Charli and Cass, thank you for bringing me happiness day in and day out with your love and energy. Thanks for the days filled with football, soccer, baseball, basketball and fun. For the journeys to and from and through preschool, grade school and middle school. Thanks for the walks to Alki, family dinners, Survivor Thursdays, the adventures at Flathead, and for the everyday moments that make my life complete.

To my mom and dad, Carole and Werner, who raised me to be strong and then helped me to remember it was so, when I needed it most. I can never thank you enough. Thank you Putz, for bringing me the peace of mind only a big brother can bring. To Honey, your letters and your spirit gave me a reason to get out of bed when I didn't want to. And to Bampa (1911-

2008) your strength and your love of writing showed me the way. Thank you.

Many thanks to Kristen Morris, who believed in my story and helped to make it a work of art. To my editor Peter Atkins, who polished my story with perfection. And to Peter Monaghan and others who read through my many drafts. Thank you.

There are so many writers who have helped me on this writing journey. Waverly Fitzgerald encouraged me when my book was only a dream. Laura Kalpakian opened my heart and mind to writing, and brought together Anna, Jennifer, Ruth, MaryLee, Betsy and Elise, of the Memoir Club, who continue to expand my knowledge of the craft. Jenny McGlothern inspires me weekly on our writing dates, in her blog and with her enthusiasm for life. And to the many hard working writers that I've met along the way that showed me that it can be done, that a dream can become a book. Amy Waeschle, Shannon Darrah, Abigail Carter and more, thank you.

Thanks to Betty, Lynn, Andrew, Sandra, Molly, Joanne and Kristy who have kept me working all these years.

To Kirsten and Leslie, my oldest and dearest friends that appreciate my nerdy side, thanks for being my silent strength. I'm so glad we were seated next to one another back in Junior High School. Thanks to Veronica and Kathy for your support through the crazy kid years. To Terry and Marilyn. And to Tim, Heidi and Rob for being perfect neighbors.

To the ballers who keep me playing, the kids that keep me sharing my love of the game, and to the coaches who continue to show me the way. Thank you!

Thank you to the doctors, nurses, police officers and therapists that saved me. A special thank you to Dr. Perry (1950-2010), thank you for putting me back together and for encouraging me to believe I could be strong again. To Dr.

Coulston for helping my parents endure the chaos. To Officer Ditmer for keeping me talking. To my nurse Jackie for her great care and for bringing boxers, Miggs and Aurora into our home. To Philip, who pushed me in physical therapy and to Moon who allowed me to relax and heal. To Janet, who guided me. And to so many others whose names are lost in the haze of trauma, I thank you for bringing me life.

A special thank you to Larry, Joan, Wendy, Vikki and Debbie for sharing Mark with me. He is forever in my heart. Thank you.